Weaving a Country

Stories from Canadian Immigrants

Wilma Maki

Pacific Educational Press
Vancouver, Canada

Published by Pacific Educational Press
Faculty of Education
University of British Columbia
Vancouver, B.C. V6T 1Z4

Telephone: 604-822-5385
Facsimile: 604-822-6603

National Library of Canada Cataloguing in Publication
   Weaving a country : stories from Canadian immigrants / [edited by] Wilma Maki.

(Alternatives to racism)
Includes index.
ISBN 1-895766-17-6

   1. Immigrants—Canada—Juvenile literature. 2. Immigrants—Canada—History—Sources—
Juvenile literature. 3. Canada—Emigration and immigration—Juvenile literature. 4. Canada—
Emigration and immigration—History—Juvenile literature. 5. Immigrants' writings, Canadian
(English) I. Maki, Wilma. II. Series.

FC104.W42 2003   j971'.0086'91   C2003-906759-9

The publisher and the Alternatives to Racism Society would like to thank the Vancouver Foundation, the Muttart Foundation, Multiculturalism and Citizenship Canada, and the University of
British Columbia Faculty of Education for their generous support of this book, and the
Department of Canadian Heritage for its ongoing support of Pacific Educational Press's
publishing program.
   Wilma Maki would like to thank all of the people who so generously shared their stories and
provided materials for this book. She would also like to extend her appreciation to the book
sponsor and to the publisher for their vision, expertise, and dedication.

Cover and inside design: Warren Clark

Front cover photographs: *clockwise from top left:* courtesy Richmond Chinese Community Soci-
ety; courtesy National Archives of Canada, PA 186957; courtesy Pauline Foggo; courtesy Town of
Pictou, Nova Scotia, Department of Recreation, Tourism and Culture.
Back cover photograph: courtesy British Columbia Archives, C-09457.

Printed in Canada

03 04 05 06   4 3 2 1

In memory of my parents and grandparents, who came to Canada from all corners of the globe,
who spoke of the richness of their origins, but not of the differences.–Wilma Maki

Contents

Introduction

In this book you will meet people from many different countries who immigrated to Canada at different times, from several hundred years ago to the present. The stories these people tell about the countries they came from, how they adapted to their new homes, the difficulties they faced, and the traditions they have contributed to Canadian culture are just a few examples of the many rich tales that make up the history of immigrants in Canada. Each story is a thread in the weaving of a country.

The book is divided into five chapters. Each chapter represents one aspect of the immigration experience. Chapter one starts with stories about why immigrants left their home country and about their journeys to a new land. Chapter two is about immigrants' first experiences in the new country, and chapter three is about the adjustments they had to make to settle in and find their new identity.

Chapter four recounts stories of groups of immigrants who experienced discrimination and prejudice in the new society, and chapter five concludes with a story that illustrates how the plants, animals, foods, and traditions immigrants have brought to Canada all contribute to the tapestry we know as Canadian culture.

The stories in this book come from many sources and in many forms: journal writing, interviews, newspaper accounts, poetry, historical fiction. We hope that this book will give you ideas about the many diverse sources you can use to search for your own family history. Voices that are not often heard—yours, your teacher's, your friends', your parents'—all are part of the weaving that makes this country's multicultural heritage. As we learn about each other's lives, we gain a deeper understanding of the contributions that all immigrants make to Canadian society.

ONE

Leaving Home

The first step of the immigration experience is leaving home. Every immigrant makes a decision to leave, prepares for the move, then journeys to the new country. In this chapter Eleanora, Susan, and Nam tell of their experiences leaving their homes.

Eleanora describes how she and her family prepared to come to Canada. They had to decide what to bring and what to leave behind; then they said their final farewells to friends and family. Susan tells us about the importance of having proper papers. Certain documents are needed to leave or enter countries and to travel between countries. Nam's story is about the dangerous journey from his homeland. Sometimes, as in Nam's case, leaving home can be life-threatening.

Immigrants have many different leaving experiences. These stories are only three threads of the Canadian fabric. During the past few centuries, people have come to Canada for many different reasons. Sometimes opportunity, dreams of freedom, or adventure have pulled them here; other times the situation in their home country has pushed them here. At home they may have experienced ethnic, racial, or religious persecution, wars, or economic hardship. Each leaving experience is different, depending on the times and the circumstances.

Despite their differences, the stories of Eleanora, Susan, and Nam show that immigrants to Canada have much in common. Each immigrant has his or her own story to tell. No matter when immigrants came to Canada, where they came from, or what they believed, their stories tell us something about ourselves or our ancestors. For all immigrants, the leaving experience was filled with good and bad, joy and sadness. No matter what lay ahead, much was left behind. And no matter what was left behind, new lives were about to start.

These stories also highlight another important point: for each immigrant who reached the shores of Canada, many did not make it. Many who wanted to come never escaped from their homeland or died in their attempts to journey to safety. For the immigrants who reached this country, Canada offered a new life and home.

As emigrants leave their country of birth, they take a final look at the land they have called home. That last glance can stir many different emotions. Emigrants who are thinking of the future might be filled with excitement and hope or, perhaps, fear and doubt. Thinking of what is left behind, they might be feeling deep sadness. Although they are leaving to live in a new place, the homeland remains a part of their life. This poem expresses one emigrant's feelings and thoughts as he catches the last glimpse of his homeland.

THE CUBAN EMIGRANT

Victor Alvarez

With the eyes red,
Looking out the window
Of an airplane
From high, too high,
You see the land in which you were born.
Then a tear goes
From your eye to your cheek.

And when you arrive
to the other land,
You will always remember
The land in which you were born.

Eleanora's Diary

ELEANORA HALLEN LIVED IN ENGLAND IN THE first half of the nineteenth century. She was one of eleven children in her family. In 1833, at age ten, she began a diary. She wrote about daily events in her life, about her family, studies, neighbourhood, social life, and pets. Two years later, in 1835, her family decided to emigrate to Canada.

In her diary, Eleanora portrays a very happy life in England. Her family was middle-class; they had servants and the children had a governess for their studies. Eleanora's father was an Anglican clergyman. The family lived in a large house named Rushock, across the street from her father's church.

Eleanora does not tell us why the Hallens decided to emigrate. The diary entries do, however, give us some clues. Eleanora mentions relatives and friends who travelled and lived in other countries. From this information we can guess it was quite usual for English people to live or work in the British colonies. In fact, the Hallens were part of what is known as the "greatest folk movement of modern times," the emigration fever of the 1800s.

People were leaving Europe, especially the British Isles, to travel to all areas of the world. Both the wealthy and the poor were flocking to North America. These people began to change the face of the continent. Before that time, North America was seen as wild bush, but opinion was changing. People started to think of it as a land of opportunity. In England it was difficult for middle- and upper-class younger sons and military officers to afford the lifestyle they were used to. For a large family such as the Hallens, a move to Canada would most likely have offered more opportunities than England could at the time.

The following excerpts from Eleanora's diary give us a picture of what many immigrants experienced before they left their home. The Hallens were breaking with a past life. Eleanora's journal describes the work and chaos involved in preparing for a move to another country.

The ship Albion *in Liverpool harbour around 1840.*

This is the journal of

Eleanora Hallen

who was born at Rushock
in the county of Worcester,
January 19, 1823

*Eleanora Hallen. 1834
December 23.*

[1833] April 1

I began to keep a journal. I am ten years old. I made
Sarah and George, my brother and sister, also Elizabeth, a cousin, April Fools; it kept me busy all morning. We expected our governess all morning, but as it
rained she did not come.

[1835] Monday, January 12

My Aunt Mary and Uncle Thomas gave us each some
money. We were all very very sorry to leave. We have
been so happy [here] . . . We shall leave Rushock the
10th of March and shall go to Perry [a relative's home]
until we leave for Canada.

Friday, January 23

We do not have school very regularly as we are so
unsettled and have a good deal of sewing to do pre-

vious to leaving for Canada. My father
. . . called on Bishop Carr. His son who
is in the army had not long arrived
from Quebec. [Father] saw a small bark
canoe that [Carr's son] had brought with
him. He lent my father a book on America.

Thursday, February 12

We all wished my Uncle Herbert good-bye. I suppose
it is the last time we shall see him in England; he was
always a very great favourite with all of us, playing
with us when children, etc.

Saturday, February 14

My father has had some blocks of wood brought, that
George may try if he can chop, against he goes to
Canada.

Wednesday, February 18

We have no school now as Miss Holmes has left and
my Father is too busy, but Sarah sometimes attends
to her Latin. A carpenter is making some large boxes
for the books as my father has a great many . . .

What to Bring from the Old Country

Emigrants had to decide what to
bring with them from the old
country. Many nineteenth-century
guidebooks listed supplies settlers
would need in Canada. The lists
were short. The Hallens brought 36
cubic hundredweight of luggage —
probably much more than they
actually needed. (One cubic
hundredweight is approximately
51 kilograms.)

The guidebooks recommended
that settlers bring items that were
either unavailable, expensive, or of
poor quality in Canada. They

suggested that settlers leave
behind heavy items that would cost
a lot to transport or could be
damaged during shipping. They
advised settlers to purchase items
required for survival, including
building or farming materials and
tools, after their arrival in Canada.

Provisions for the Voyage

By law, ships transporting
emigrants were to provide food for
passengers. In 1830, ships provided
bread, beer, meat, vegetables,
cocoa, sugar, and tea. William

Cattermole, the author of the 1831
guidebook *Emigration,* suggested
that passengers bring extra
provisions, such as meat, bread,
flour, and soup. He also suggested
bringing "a pig or two, and if
possible, a sheep. Many take fowls
but they often become sick. Ducks,
however, do well. Herring, salt fish,
eggs, suet, butter, rice, onions and
carrots, with a few apples for
puddings . . . are the main foods
wanted."

A 1855 guidebook, *The
Canadian Settler's Guide,* by

Tuesday, March 17

Elizabeth and I routed out the bags and sorted them out and made them in little bundles. I got all of my clothes together and my mother pinned them up . . . The bags are in a great rumpus and so we had a great heap of old rubbish and stuff. My mother says perhaps the servants will like to have a few things.

Friday, March 20

My mother thought she could go up to Rushock because [today] the auctioneer is going to take the catalogue. When we came there, the auctioneer Mr. Cole was come. He was [listing] the downstairs things. The things were all in a bustle; the study was buried with things which are not going to be sold.

Tuesday, March 24

My mother is very busy. The beds are to be packed. The buds are coming out upon the trees; I am afraid we never shall see the chestnut tree in its bloom again nor our pretty garden.

Thursday, March 26

Anne Jackson and Sally scoured all the tin things . . . Sarah, Mary and I washed all the glass. We took it in turns to nurse the baby . . . It is very sorrowful to see the things lying about because I know we shall never see them in order again.

Friday, March 27

We are going to have a wagon from Mr. John Letts of Cake Boll tomorrow. It is a very busy day today.

Saturday, March 28

The beds were all packed up and nearly all the things went except a few in the study. The wagon was heaped up very high.

Sunday, March 29

We none of us went to church. My Aunts did. We did not go because our things are not unpacked.

Monday, March 30

All our things are in the apple room and at the top of

A wood engraving of emigrants leaving England, published in 1849 in the London Journal.

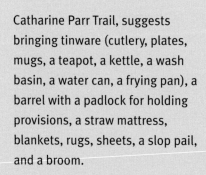

Catharine Parr Trail, suggests bringing tinware (cutlery, plates, mugs, a teapot, a kettle, a wash basin, a water can, a frying pan), a barrel with a padlock for holding provisions, a straw mattress, blankets, rugs, sheets, a slop pail, and a broom.

Furniture

The guidebooks recommended that the emigrants not bring furniture. Freight costs, storage, and duty made transporting furniture expensive, and there was a risk of damage. John Howison, who wrote *Sketches of Upper Canada* (1821), suggested, "Everything that is necessary for the log-hut can be bought in the settlement. Good furniture is not suited to the rude housing of the new immigrants."

Clothes

The guidebooks did recommend bringing clothes. Clothing was not yet manufactured in Canada, so it was very expensive. The emigrants were advised to bring a supply of

the landing. We cleared the landing a little . . . The sale is at Rushock today.

Wednesday, April 1

My Father, Edgar and I went to Rushock; it looks very desolate.

Wednesday, April 29

We had our breakfast very early and then Mary and I got the children ready. Mrs. Beverley went with us, the children went in a . . . coach [to Liverpool]. We went in a boat to the ship, which is lying in the river. She is a beautiful ship, the largest in Liverpool. She is a Merchantman. There are upwards of three hundred persons on board, including the crew. There is no cow on board; there are two sheep and three pigs.

Thursday, April 30

My Grandpapa, Uncle William [and some] other clergymen came to take leave of us . . . At 12 o' clock, a favourable breeze springing up, we weighed anchor. I felt regret as I saw Liverpool gradually fading from sight.

Although they left much behind, the Hallens brought many aspects of their old life with them. In Canada their work and surroundings were rustic compared to England. They still had time, however, to keep up their traditions: studies, hobbies, pets, and especially social activities.

The Hallen family settled in the Simcoe district north of Toronto. They moved into a log home that they named "Rushock" after their home in England. Coming to Canada allowed them to buy property, which they could not afford in England, and they began farming. In 1840, Mr. Hallen got a job as a chaplain at the army base in the nearby town of Penetanguishene. Their new lives were not free of great losses, however. The baby in the family died a few years after they arrived. Eleanora died at the age of twenty-three from tuberculosis.

clothes, cotton cloth, and shoes. Catharine Parr Trail's *The Canadian Settler's Guide* recommended flannel cloth: "Nothing can be more suitable to the climate and the work of the Canadian settler's wife or daughter than the gowns made of this country flannel. It is very durable, lasting often two or three seasons. When worn out as a working dress, it makes good sleigh-quilts for travelling or can be cut up into rag-carpets."

Tools

The guidebooks recommended buying tools in Canada. Tools were available in most places, and buying them close to the new home would cut transportation costs.

Animals

Cattermole's guidebook, *Emigration*, suggested bringing sheep or horses. Both animals would do well in Canada, but great care would be needed during the voyage. Also, "a few English grey rabbits . . . keep them and raise a stock . . . The fur could be sent home or to the States. The carcass could be sold in town."

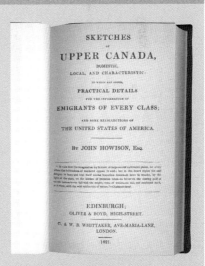

The title page of a book originally published in London, England, in 1821.

SUSAN'S VISA

SUSAN BLUMAN WAS BORN IN 1920 AND GREW UP in Warsaw, Poland, where her family had lived for many generations. They were Jewish, and they were happy in Warsaw until the start of World War II in the fall of 1939.

During the war, there was a very strong anti-Jewish movement in Germany. The Nazis, who were in power there, wanted to rid Germany of Jewish people. As country after country in Europe came under German control, Jewish people were afraid for their lives and many tried to escape. However, anyone crossing an international border usually needs a visa, which is a piece of paper showing that the person carrying it has permission to travel between countries. During World War II, it was impossible to travel without a visa and it was very difficult for a Jewish person to obtain one. For Susan and her husband, Nathan, getting visas meant the difference between life and death.

Here, Susan describes the difficulties she and Nathan had in getting visas and how they finally escaped from Europe.

Life in Warsaw became more and more difficult. There was constant German bombardment. My sister was wounded. It became difficult to get food and water. Poland [had] surrendered and the Germans occupied the city. My brother, my boyfriend Nathan, and his brother fled to eastern Poland, which was under Russian occupation.

It was no longer safe to be a Jew under the new Nazi government. My father, who could easily be identified as a Jew because of his beard, could no longer go out. I was sent to get the food rations. One day, waiting in a line-up for food, I saw some Polish

Jewish families are forced to evacuate an apartment building in the Warsaw ghetto in April–May 1943.

people denouncing Jews to the Nazis. I was outraged. I had always thought of myself as a Polish citizen just like them. We began to hear rumours that all Jews were going to be forced to live in a ghetto.

An acquaintance brought me a letter from Nathan, urging me to join him in eastern Poland. My father allowed me to go on condition that I come back in two weeks. Nathan's sister and I left with our packsacks. My father gave me his belt with four American dollars in it. I still have that belt. We met Nathan and my brother. My father sent me a message asking me to return right away, but I didn't listen. I married Nathan a few days later on December 26, 1939.

Nathan and I fled to Lithuania. We had to walk for miles in deep snow. As we had little money, Nathan

A reproduction of Susan's passport.

got a job teaching agriculture to Hashomair Hatzair, a Jewish youth group preparing to emigrate to Palestine. I got a job doing some sewing.

ONE MAN MAKES A DIFFERENCE

In Lithuania many Jewish refugees were able to get visas at the Japanese consulate because of the actions of one individual, Chiune Sugihara. A visa is an important piece of paper, but behind each visa is a person.

Chiune Sugihara was Japanese, born in a samurai family. He studied English at university, paying for his education working on the docks and as a tutor. After his studies, he wanted to see the world, so he joined the Foreign Ministry. He was posted in China and then in Finland. As war approached, the Japanese government transferred him to Kaunas, Lithuania, to open a one-person consulate.

When Russia closed all the embassies in Lithuania in 1940, Consul Sugihara asked for an extension to stay. He became the only foreign consul in Kaunas. Since the Dutch consulate had closed, the Jewish refugees begged him for exit visas. He wired his government three times for permission to issue visas to the Jewish refugees. The government refused each time. This is what the government wired:

CONCERNING TRANSIT VISAS REQUESTED PREVIOUSLY STOP ADVISE ABSOLUTELY NOT TO BE ISSUED ANY TRAVELER NOT HOLDING FIRM END VISA WITH GUARANTEED DEPARTURE EX JAPAN STOP

NO EXCEPTIONS STOP

NO FURTHER INQUIRIES EXPECTED STOP

K TANAKA FOREIGN MINISTRY

We had heard of a way to leave Europe. The Dutch consulate in Lithuania would stamp our passports to allow us to emigrate to a tiny Dutch colony in the Caribbean. If we got that stamp, the Japanese consulate would give us a transit visa. If we had the Japanese transit visa, the Russians would allow us to travel through Russia out of Europe. But we were too late. Russia had ordered all foreign consulates to leave Lithuania in July 1940.

We then heard of a Japanese consul who was willing to issue Japanese transit visas. Thousands of desperate Jewish refugees surrounded his consulate. We were among the last to be seen before the consulate closed in September. Even without a Dutch stamp, the consul gave us a Japanese transit visa. We were overjoyed.

We travelled by train to Moscow. Then we took the Trans-Siberian railway for twelve days to Vladivostok, an eastern port city in Russia. From there

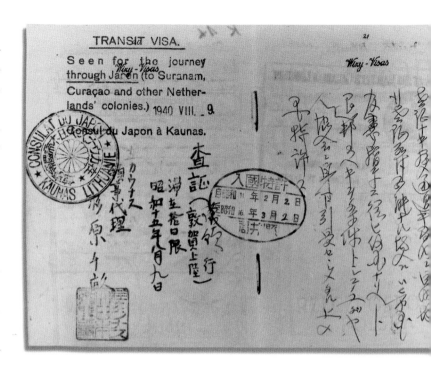

A typical transit visa for travel to Dutch colonies via Japan. This one was issued by Consul Chiune Sugihara in 1940.

Consul Sugihara and his family, along with German soldiers, in front of the Japanese consulate in Konigsberg, Germany in 1940.

When Consul Sugihara received the wire, he had to make a decision: obey his superiors or help the refugees. Helping them would mean going against Nazi policies. That could endanger his and his family's lives. He and his wife finally decided that they had no choice: he would issue the visas. From July to early September, he sat for endless hours, writing out by hand as many

we boarded a Japanese boat for Tzuruga in Japan and then on to Kobe. A Jewish service organization found us accommodation. About fifteen of us slept in one room. The Japanese treated us very well. We wrote to my parents and sent them parcels of tea and sausages. My parents wrote back saying how worried they were about us. I still have their letters.

The transit visas did not allow us to stay in Japan for long. The Polish consulate in Japan had received twenty-five Canadian visas for professional men for the period of the war. Nathan was an agriculture engineer so he qualified. But I didn't. We went to Tokyo and managed to convince them to give me a visa. We got it twenty-four hours before the ship left. In 1941, after six months in Japan, we sailed from Yokohama to Vancouver. I was nineteen years old. I couldn't believe it when we finally arrived in Canada.

After Susan left Europe, the Jewish people in Warsaw were placed in one confined area called the Warsaw Ghetto. Later, many of these Jews and hundreds of thousands of others, throughout Europe, were placed in concentration camps and murdered. This assault on the Jewish people is called the Holocaust. It is estimated that up to six million Jews died during the Holocaust. One and a half million children died, almost 90 percent of the Jewish children in Europe. This is the horror Susan left behind. Both Susan and Nathan lost all of their family.

Compared to the number of Jews who died, the number who managed to escape Europe was small. Only a few Jews managed to get visas to Canada. Although they entered Canada on temporary visas, Susan and Nathan were able to become Canadian citizens after the war ended. They settled in Vancouver, British Columbia, and raised three children.

Consul Sugihara started writing visas early in the morning and continued till nighttime, stopping only for dinner. He wrote them for more than a month.

as 300 visas a day. The Japanese government ordered him to leave Kaunas.

Chiune Sugihara eventually ended up working in the diplomatic service in Romania. In 1944, he and his family were arrested by the Russians, and they spent the next two years in an internment camp. When they finally returned to Japan, the Japanese government dismissed him from diplomatic service. He was disgraced.

It was not until 1969 that one of the refugees who had received a visa in Lithuania found Mr. Sugihara. In 1985, the Yad Vashem (the Holocaust Memorial) and Heroes' Remembrance Authority in Jerusalem recognized Mr. Sugihara as "Righteous Among Nations." It is estimated that his act of humanitarianism saved as many as 10,000 people from certain death.

NAM'S JOURNEY TO CANADA

NAM WAS TEN YEARS OLD IN 1979. HE LIVED ON A farm in Vietnam with his brothers, sisters, and parents. His family had lived on the farm for many generations. They worked hard and lived in humble surroundings. Nam's father worked part-time as a carpenter and his mother worked in a nearby coal mine.

One morning Nam's father told Nam and his sister, Ling, that they had to leave in one hour for the coast. Because of increasing political problems in Vietnam, Nam's father was sending Nam and his sister out of the country to safety. In 1979, the people of Vietnam were living in the turmoil of war's aftermath. For twenty years, Vietnam had been involved in a civil war. The United States was also involved in this war. The war had ended in 1975, but there was still chaos in the country. Tens of thousands of people were fleeing Vietnam. They hoped to get to refugee camps and from there to distant countries where they could find peace. All the money Nam's father had saved went to buy passage for the two children.

Nam and Ling walked all day to the harbour. That night, they boarded an old wooden boat, the *Ho Chi Minh*. On the boat, to Nam's surprise, he found his cousin Kon Ki. Two hundred and fifteen people crowded on the boat before it set out on the South China Sea. On the voyage, the *Ho Chi Minh* would be robbed by pirates and later run into a storm. Here is a description of what Nam experienced during and after the *Ho Chi Minh* battled the storm. The excerpt is from the book *A Boy Called Nam*, by Canadian author Leo Heaps.

Vietnamese refugees aboard one of many boats in the China Sea. They became known as "boat people" because many had to be rescued from overcrowded and unsafe boats.

Refugees were lucky to find any space to sleep on the overcrowded boats from Vietnam.

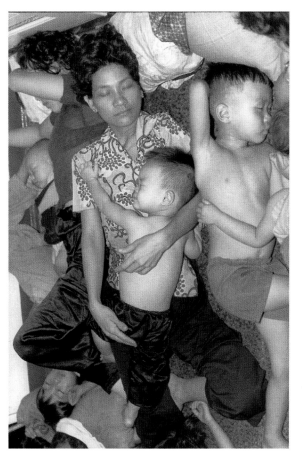

The overloaded boat was so low in the water that the green waves of the South China Sea rolled completely over it. In the hold the refugees were tossed ceaselessly about so that no one could sleep or eat. Food and belongings swished around the bottom of the boat in the rising bilge water . . . The sea poured in faster than it could be pumped overboard.

On the third morning of the storm Nam again crept up the ladder and pushed open the hatch. This time he was followed by Ling and Kon Ki. To their amazement the deck was almost swept clean. The cabin, with the captain and the mate . . . and the two life boats had all been washed overboard. The Ho Chi Minh . . . wallowed at the mercy of wave and wind.

Nam was certain the end of the world had come. By this time, the water in the bottom of the boat was waist-deep. Nam, Ling, and Kon Ki crawled carefully forward over the leaking deck in search of planks to which they could cling when the ship went down as it

A Letter Home

Refugees who escaped war-torn Vietnam often left many loved ones behind. The separation would have been especially difficult for children who were sent away without their parents. Living in Vietnam was dangerous, and young boys were often taken into the army. Some parents were able to send away only a few of their children. Many of these children went to strange countries and knew nothing of the fate of their families at home.

Garry Son Hoan boarded a small fishing boat in November 1978. He was nine years old. He left with his sisters, Muy Shing and My Chou, and his brother-in-law, Liang. From the fishing boat they boarded a large freighter, the *Hai Hong*. The refugees on the vessel spent many weeks at sea before they were allowed to land in Malaysia. From there Garry and his sisters came to Canada. Canada took 604 refugees from the *Hai Hong*.

Many things were different and sometimes strange for Garry when he came to his new home. He wished to tell his mother about these things. He did not know where his mother was, but he wrote letters to her anyway. This letter gives some of his first impressions. It is from the book *Letter to Vietnam*, by Eugene Buia.

Dear Mother,
We have been in so many places. Once we left the fishing boat and went on the Hai Hong *we thought*

surely would do. Pieces of rope and planks that had broken loose floated over the half-submerged deck. Kon Ki tied Nam and his sister to one of the pieces of wood and himself to another. Then they gradually slithered towards the ship's wheel, held onto it, and waited.

On the third night the storm was at its height. The Ho Chi Minh *suddenly began to break apart . . . A monstrous wave towered momentarily above the deck like a mountain and then thundered down, tearing the boat in half.*

Nam saw the last great wave strike the vessel just before he was swept into the sea with his sister. The Ho Chi Minh *had disintegrated into a mass of broken wood and screaming men, women, and children . . .*

The South China Sea was suddenly warm and deserted. The cries of the helpless refugees had faded and been replaced by a great lonely calm. Together

A small boat with 162 Vietnamese refugees on board sank a short distance from shore. Most of the people were rescued and reached the coast safely.

we were saved, but many times we came to land and many times we were sent back out on the water again. I am very tired of moving but it doesn't stop. Always we are waiting to go someplace else, but here in Canada, for the first time, I feel safe, almost as safe as in Saigon with you.

We came to an army base called Longue Pointe. I must tell you the first thing I noticed was that this land is colder than anyplace I have ever been. We were taken to a large building to get jackets and pants. They are funny clothes that make me look fat, but they are very warm.

The planes and the soldiers of Base Longue Pointe and all the men asking questions remind me of Saigon. When the planes take off sometimes it sounds like the shells fired at Saigon and I jump, but everyone says we are safe now. The streets in this army base are quiet and Liang says we might never hear shooting again. That seems impossible, but none of the ladies or men here are hurt. I asked Liang if there was war here too. He said no. I wonder if these men and

ladies have ever heard guns.

Do my friends wonder where I am? Have you told them? I wish I could have. I kept it a secret as you told me to. I hope you can bring some of my friends with you when you come. Can you bring my dog, Ry? You would like it here. No more shooting.

Love,
Garry Son Hoan
P.S. This is my new Canadian name. I like it very much. I heard it in a movie.

Nam and Ling held on to their plank of wood, the ropes that had once bound them gone.

Ling scarcely spoke except to occasionally utter a sentence, always on the same subjects. She thought of her home. And she wondered if anyone would ever find them.

"Will a ship come to save us?" Ling asked in a whisper.

"Yes," Nam always answered. "Yes, a ship will come. I promise, someone will find us."

Many pieces of wood from the boat drifted by them but they did not see anyone else, living or dead. Ling no longer sobbed. Although she still clung with a tight grip to the plank, her face had become very white and she could barely whisper. All she said was that she was very tired and would like to sleep. Nam knew he must not let her go to sleep for fear that she would not awaken again. He sang songs he remembered from his babyhood and regularly poked her with his finger, refusing to allow her to close her eyes. The wind died on the children's second night in the sea.

A Vietnamese family that is happily resettled in Vancouver.

With the new dawn the wind faded away altogether. Nam was vaguely aware that the storm was over and that he was still alive. When he turned to speak to his sister, his heart suddenly filled with horror. Ling was gone. Some time in the dark while Nam had fitfully dozed, Ling had silently sunk beneath the waves. Nam was too weak to cry. He only choked on the sobs that silently rose in his throat. He wondered, too, what had become of Kon Ki.

The warm, bright sun now beat down like a whip on the peaceful water. Across the flat water he could see for many miles to the horizon in every direction. Nam dreamed as he drifted alone more dead than alive on the sea . . . All of his earlier life seemed so far away and yet so clear. He wondered if he were in heaven. He watched several large white sharks that flashed just below the water. They soon left him in favour of other prey, the many corpses that floated not far away. The sun turned the flat sea into a shining, silver mirror.

Nam eventually was rescued by a small fishing junk. He was brought to Macao, an island off the coast of Hong Kong, the only survivor of the *Ho Chi Minh*. In Macao, Nam met Leo Heaps, who was in Hong Kong at the time helping refugees. Nam eventually settled in Vancouver, British Columbia, with the Heaps family. He adjusted quickly to his new life and learned to enjoy North American pastimes such as baseball and skiing. One night a call came from Beijing, China. It was from his father. The family had escaped to a camp in China and all were safe.

Many Vietnamese, like Nam, fled their homeland fearing for their lives. The journey itself was often dangerous, but the people were so desperate that they would try to escape by any means possible. It is estimated that a quarter of a million Vietnamese drowned at sea and thousands of others were killed by pirates during and after the war in Vietnam. The lucky ones, like Nam, made it safely to other countries, including Canada.

TWO

Adjusting to Canada

When immigrants first come to Canada, they are faced with many differences between their past life and their new one. There are differences in climate, environment, customs, language, and ideas. The newly arrived must adjust to fit in. In this chapter, you will read stories about early Scots and Sikhs, and hear from two individuals, Ernie and Jane. All of them take their first steps towards making a home in a new land.

Sometimes Canada forces changes on the new immigrant. The land and climate itself demand immediate attention. So it was for the Scots. They found Canada a different and hostile land and had to learn new ways to find food and shelter in order to survive. The Sikhs met another kind of hostile environment. The people of Canada did not want them in the country. This reality forced different kinds of adjustment for the new Sikh immigrants.

Although new immigrants are forced to change in some ways, each immigrant can make his or her own choices about other changes. The stories of Ernie and Jane tell about their individual choices. Ernie decided to learn quickly how to become one of the group. Jane had to decide between joining groups in the new country or staying in her ethnic community that was already established in Canada.

The immigration experience requires many kinds of adjustment. Sometimes change is for survival. Other times it is for harmony, and yet other times it is a matter of individual choice. Sometimes change affects the original culture in devastating ways; other times the immigrant wants to forget the past. Change can be an exciting and wonderful experience. It can also be difficult and confusing. Often it is very lonely, as the new life also requires an adjustment to separation from loved ones.

Adjustments differ greatly between groups and individuals. When immigrants come, what country they come from, and how other Canadians feel about them all affect the adjustments of newcomers. There have been difficult times for every group, no matter what religion or race. Each has had to face some kind of trial.

Immigrants face unusual and unfamiliar surroundings on arrival in Canada. The new environment can be exciting or difficult. Sometimes the immigrants learn about the new culture and climate from others, but many times they learn on their own. In this poem an immigrant from Sri Lanka tells about his first meeting with ice and how, over time, he adjusted and progressed.

FROM SHOVEL TO SELF-PROPELLED SNOW BLOWER: THE IMMIGRANT'S PROGRESS

Rienzi Crusz

*Two days into the Promised Land
and my eyes dance:
Supermarket and Mall,
I am in TV's arms.
No one can mention the forecast: tomorrow
100% precipitation / freezing rain.
So down the shimmering street I go
with only my sun head and ADIDAS,
to learn how the feet suddenly slide, shudder
with instant pain,
the body lumps to horizontal woe.
3 broken ribs, some hefty pain.
I've learned the beatitudes of ice,
something sacred, something cold,
demanding respect.*

*After twenty winters in my bones,
shovelling my sidewalk snow,
a self-propelled snow blower I've called Pablo
now does my chores,
    vertical as my front door,
and I am happy.*

THE PICTOU COUNTY HIGHLANDERS' FIRST YEAR

Some time early in the month [September 1773] the Hector *entered the Gulf of St. Lawrence and Northumberland Strait and, finally, crept past Pictou's sandbar and into the wide and beautiful harbour. Tradition has it that the day was bright with autumn sunshine. The date was September 15.*

THIS IS HOW DONALD MACKAY, THE AUTHOR OF *Scotland Farewell*, describes the arrival of the ship *Hector* to Pictou Harbour on the northeastern coast of present-day Nova Scotia. Aboard the ship were 179 Scottish immigrants. They were mostly Highlanders from central and west Scotland. They were the first of a large-scale emigration of Scots to settle in Nova Scotia.

Each Highlander came hoping for a new and better life. But these early immigrants, like many new immigrants, experienced a great shock. The new land was nothing like they had been told or had imagined. The Highlanders were coming to farm. They had responded to advertisements selling farm country in Acadia.

An advertisement in the Edinburgh Advertiser *in Scotland in 1773.*

For **PICTOU HARBOUR** in Nova Scotia, **BOSTON** and **FALMOUTH** in New England.

THE Ship HECTOR, John Speir mafter, burthen 200 tons, now lying in the harbour of GREENOCK. For freight or paffage apply to John Pagan merchant in Glafgow, Lee, Tucker, and Co. merchants in Greenock; and in order to accommodate all paffengers that may offer, the fhip will wait until the 10th of May next, but will pofitively fail betwixt and the 15th of that month.

N.B. Pictou harbour lyes directly oppofite to the ifland of St. John's, at the diftance of 15 miles only.

At the time, huge tracts of land were granted to individuals or to companies to develop. The landowners in Pictou had described the area to the Highlanders in glowing terms. It was rich for farming, had plenty of game and fish, and was situated on a harbour. It was near a settled area, the Island of St. John (now called Prince Edward Island). The owners offered cheap ship passage, a berth, and food on the voyage. They promised provisions for one year and accommodation once the settlers landed. The offer sounded promising to those on the *Hector*.

When the Highlanders landed, they discovered, to their dismay, conditions that were very different from what they had imagined. The dark forests were unknown and threatening to them. They were exhausted and hungry from the difficult journey crossing the Atlantic. And the ship had arrived too late for them to plant crops to harvest before winter set in.

They had much to learn to survive the oncoming winter, and they had to adjust quickly. Donald MacKay is one of the descendants of the Hector group. Here, MacKay describes some of the experiences of the new settlers.

None of the Highlanders on the Hector *left any record of how they felt as they lined the rails to stare at the shore. It must have seemed as wild to them as Africa. They would have seen a few scattered homes in little clearings in the forest and some of the earlier settlers hurrying toward them through the trees. The Highlanders' brave show of salt-stained plaids, broadswords, and bagpipes could only have stirred the pity of the settlers who came to greet them.*

From the start, the Highlanders found great hardship at Pictou Harbour . . . The "Americans," as the earlier settlers were called, tried to help the immigrants with fresh food, sympathy and good advice, but their own resources were lean. The harvest they were gathering from among the tree stumps was barely enough for themselves. The Hector *was to drop off enough supplies to last the winter on her return voyage from the southern colonies, but for now the only food was that which the earlier settlers could spare.*

The Highlanders had come expecting farmland which at least looked like the fertile land they had known at home. But here, except for a few stump-ridden patches, there was nothing but unbroken forest, and such a forest as none had seen in their own bare hills. When they saw the Indians watching them from the shelter of the forest they worried about the safety of their families, unaware that the Micmacs had fled at the sound of the pipes . . .

The newcomers' reaction to the forest was one of dread. All their lives they had lived in wide, open spaces and what they had known as "deer forests" had hardly any trees at all. They were superstitious people. They envisioned such dark places with a host of terrors, and for a generation and more their fear of the woods was a theme which ran through their folklore.

The hardwood hills behind them were turning red and yellow, the nights sharp and chill. They had been promised accommodation until they could build homes of their own, but again they were disappointed. They were warned to hurry in their work lest winter catch them without a shelter. Most had never seen a log house before or had the slightest idea of how to build one. They had no skill with the woodsman's axe, for their tools at home had been the hoe or the crooked spade. The experienced colonists had to teach them how to fell big trees without killing themselves.

The Highlanders met with one problem after another . . . Small groups began to drift to established communities in the area. Only 60 or 70 people remained in rough lean-tos roofed with bark and branches.

Those that remained spent a miserable winter learning the painful lessons of survival. They learned

Do You Have the Gaelic?

Highlanders come from the central and western parts of Scotland. They are mainly Celtic in origin and until recently spoke Gaelic. With the coming of the Highlanders to Canada, Gaelic became a common language in the new country. In the beginning of the nineteenth century, Gaelic was the third most common language spoken. By mid-century communities of Gaelic speakers were established in Nova Scotia, particularly in Cape Breton, Pictou, and Antigonish, and in parts of Prince Edward Island, New Brunswick, and Ontario.

Today few people still speak Gaelic. Only a few thousand, mainly in Cape Breton, keep the language alive in Canada. Losing Gaelic was part of the adjustment immigrants made. Here, Joe Neil MacNeil of Big Pond, Cape Breton Island, tells of growing up in a Gaelic-speaking community. Gaelic had an oral tradition of song, poetry, and storytelling. This tradition was part of everyday social life. Joe laments that the language is dying out with the older generation.

I was adopted at the age of six months by a couple living in Middle Cape. They were quite elderly and couldn't speak a word of English, and so it was that I grew up knowing only Gaelic. When I started school I had no English of course, except for a few words here and there. I was taught how to say my name in English and I was able to remember that, but that was about it. The funny part of it was that I could read a bit of English, but couldn't speak it.

At school we didn't use Gaelic except when we were outside playing. Inside the school Gaelic was forbidden despite the fact that most of the children spoke it as a

to dig up large quantities of clams and cover them with sand before the snow fell so they could be dug up during the winter as needed; they learned to fish through the harbour ice, to clothe themselves to protect their hands and faces from frostbite, to pile large stacks of wood beside their shelters to keep the fires constantly burning. These lessons were frequently costly. Metal utensils were practically irreplaceable, and when a cast-iron pot cracked in the cold night when left outside with water in it, they lamented the loss but rarely left their pots outside again.

By Christmas week the snow was blowing through the cracks and crannies in their lean-tos, and by the last week of December there was a foot of snow. They received unexpected help from the Indians, who brought them meat from the hunt from time to time and showed them how to use snowshoes . . .

Despite the constant hardship, the naivete of the Highlanders was sometimes humorous, even to themselves. Since it was winter, they had seen no bears, but had been warned about them by the settlers. One day a Highlander, concluding that a strange-looking animal near the camp must be the dreaded bear, sounded the alarm and roused his neighbours. Surprised at finding that bears were so small, he fired nine shots before killing the beast. Examining it, the Highlanders hurt their fingers, for no one had told them that bears had quills. When spring came they had ample opportunity to distinguish bears from porcupines.

For some the mosquitoes were worse than bears. One settler braved the winter only to flee the place in summer, calling the mosquitoes a plague from God. Less alarming were the Highlanders' encounters with the flora. Having heard that sugar came from trees, one woman, pulling off bark and chewing it early that winter, was disappointed in the taste. The settlers explained to her there would be no syrup for many

first language. This was around 1914 or '15, and English had already made enough inroads that most families around there could speak both, although they preferred Gaelic. The parents and the younger children were picking up what English they had from the older children who were bringing it home from school.

Little by little I learned the English language but it took a long time. In spite of this I never lost my love for the beautiful Gaelic and for the customs which my own people had brought over from the Hebrides. Stories were a big part of the social life back then, especially in the long dark night of winter. No people in particular would be invited to a house-visit. They would just drop by and they were always welcome. Some excelled at singing songs and others at reciting poems. Still others were outstanding musicians and dancers. I was most interested in the storytellers, the ones who could keep you spellbound by reciting the tales

A painting of a house in Pictou, Nova Scotia in 1817. Gaelic was widely spoken in Pictou County, Cape Breton Island, and Antigonish in the nineteenth century.

that had been passed down from generation to generation over hundreds of years.

weeks. By late February the snow had turned to rain, the streams began to flow and the harbour lost its ice. They soon learned that syrup really did come from maple trees, and when the sap stopped running they tied stout withes around the trees and tried to squeeze out more.

Spring had come and the Highlanders had survived their first winter. It had been a difficult beginning in a new land. The rich rolling farmland did not exist. They were faced with an environment they knew nothing about. In time, however, they did learn. That spring they moved up the rivers that fed into the harbour and began to clear their land. They had an enormous task ahead.

The Highlanders had been bitterly disappointed when they arrived. Many left, but some stayed. Two years later, two dozen families and single men from the *Hector* were still in the Pictou area. Others from their homeland joined them. A decade after the arrival of the *Hector*, the population had grown to 500. By the 1830s, the whole township had a population of 10,000 Scots. The town of Pictou had 1,500 people, 200 buildings, and an export trade in shipbuilding, fish, coal, and some timber.

The *Hector* immigrants' dream was not waiting for them; they had to make it themselves from the dreaded forests. But they eventually succeeded, and Canada became their home. An immigrant poet, John Maclean, wrote, "A hidden grief has overfilled me since I've been doomed to stagnate here for the rest of my life with little amusement in the gnarled forest, and without anyone to ask me if I'd sing a song." Later, he wrote, "Canada is our country. The new land of freedom and plenty."

The Scots kept many of their old ways, but the ways of the New World became part of their life as they adjusted to Canada.

A replica of the ship Hector *was constructed at the Hector Heritage Quay, Pictou, Nova Scotia. It was launched on September 16, 2000.*

VOICES OF PIONEER SIKHS

IN THE NORTHERN PART OF INDIA LIES THE province of Punjab. The province is home to a minority group of people called the Sikhs. About 15 million Sikhs live in India—a mere 2 percent of the total population. The Sikh religion, founded about 500 years ago, gives this group their distinct identity.

Sikhs starting coming to Canada in the early 1900s. Some of their experiences have been recorded by Sarjeet Singh Jagpal in his book *Becoming Canadians*. Sarjeet was born in Mission, British Columbia, and is a descendant of one of the early settlers. Because the Sikhs have an oral culture, Sarjeet decided to tape the stories of the older immigrants as a record for future generations.

Like many other newcomers to Canada, the Sikhs had to adjust to a new language, customs, and climate. But the group had other trials as well. In the early 1900s, anti-Asian feelings were reflected in both government laws and in the general population. The government severely limited Sikh immigration. Between 1908 and 1920, less than 150 Sikhs were allowed into the country. Only nine women were allowed in from 1904 to 1920. These restrictions affected Sikh immigrants' lives, work, and behaviour, and meant that the early Sikh community was virtually all male. These restrictions also affected the immigrants' reaction to the Canadian environment.

The Sikhs had to adjust to the prejudice. They made an attempt not to stand out and be different, which sometimes meant going against their religious beliefs. Not only were they away from their families, they had to immediately become involved in a struggle for equal and fair treatment, which became a major part of their adjustment to Canada. The immigrant Sikhs of the 1920s

Sikh immigrants from India arriving in Vancouver in the early 1900s. Almost no Sikh women were allowed into Canada at that time.

chose to make changes. Sikhs who had come before helped them. Community life of the gurdwara (temple) was central for the early Sikh community. Housing, employment, and heath and welfare, as well as financial support for Sikh causes, were all taken care of at the gurdwara.

Here are the voices of some Sikh immigrants. The stories Sarjeet recorded tell of adjusting to life in Canada in the 1920s and '30s. The Sikhs were just being joined by their wives and children and were trying to fit into a still-unfriendly environment.

MR. MANGA S. JAGPAL: When our boat was still out in the harbour and we approached the city of Victoria, I thought what kind of a place is this? I didn't see any farms or crops, just forest, like a jungle. Where do they get their food? What am I going to do in such a poor country? All I saw were trees, I couldn't see any big buildings yet, just tiny little shacks.

MR. DARSHAN S. SANGHA: When we arrived in Victoria, the workers began to unload the cargo from the front of the ship. They were unloading heavy things. It was the month of March and the workers wore navy blue coveralls made of denim and thick wool jackets. They were struggling with the heavy loads and their clothes were filthy from their labouring. This was the first time in my life that I had seen white people working like this; everywhere I had been in India and along the way, coloured people did all the work. This was very strange to me, I couldn't believe it. I asked my uncle who these people were. He said they are goras [white people], they are Canadians.

MR. GURBACHAN S. JOHL: When I came in 1921, there were no boys in this area. Two boys lived in Abbotsford . . . Then when four of us boys landed together the Canadian Sikhs were so happy. They kept saying, "Our boys, our boys." They couldn't do enough for us. I

EARLY SIKHS AND THE LUMBER BUSINESS

The West Coast forest gave immigrant Sikhs their livelihoods. At some stage in his life, every early Sikh male immigrant, educated or not, would work in the lumber mills. They would live in a bunkhouse and eat in a cookhouse.

Most of the immigrants of 1904 to 1908 found employment in the False Creek lumber mills in Vancouver, British Columbia. It was in this area, therefore, that they built their first gurdwara and where some bought property. The Sikhs also began to work in mills in different parts of British Columbia.

The largest community of workers was at the Fraser Mills in New Westminster. According to one Sikh, there were between two hundred and three hundred Sikh workers there in 1925. All were single men, with the exception of two families. There were bunk-houses for the men, each housing thirty to fifty people. There were also four to five cookhouses. The company had built a temple for the workers in 1908. However, it paid the Sikhs five cents less per hour than it paid white workers.

The living and cooking areas at the mills were managed by the Sikhs themselves. At the mills, the cookhouses were separate. Usually, they were managed and run by elder Sikhs or men who were not employed. These men would prepare the food, and the Sikh workers would in turn pay them. When new immigrants came, the older ones would help them find jobs. They would go from one mill to the next until a job was found. If money was needed, they loaned it to the newcomer.

Another mill in which Sikhs worked, Sooke Lake, was owned by a Sikh. By 1920 some of the early Sikh settlers had established their own businesses in lumber. One Sikh family, the Singh Johl brothers, started a wood-hauling business.

felt so much love for these people, they treated us so well. Whenever I went to the Second Avenue gurdwara, they treated me so special. The first time I stood in line to eat roti in the langar [eating hall], one old-timer took me by an arm and took me in to the centre of the hall in front of everybody. He said to me, "My son, we want you to serve us roti so that all of us can get to see and meet you. You'll get to know us and we'll get to know you." When I went around serving the roti, they made me feel so special. They were such loving people.

MRS. PARITAM K. SANGHA: On the day that I arrived in 1932, my husband took me to the shop to get new clothes right away. I pleaded with him that I hadn't had anything to eat and that I was starving, but he did not listen. First, we got the new dresses, then later we got something to eat. It was the rule then to dress like the white ladies and keep our hair covered with a scarf at all times.

MRS. PRITAM K. JOHL: When we stopped in Hong Kong I bought some dresses. Everybody said that we couldn't land unless we dressed properly. The pioneers insisted that we dress like the other Canadian people. They would not let anyone dress differently; we had to show that we could fit in and be just like the white people.

MR. MAWA S. MANGAT: My dad made me cut my hair. Right after I got off the ship he took me to the Japanese barber at Fraser Mills. I cried all the way through it, [and] I couldn't sleep for a couple of nights. I'll never forget that.

MR. KULDEEP S. BAINS: My two brothers were working at Sooke Lake in the sawmill. They came to see me the day after I landed in Victoria. First thing in the morning, Bunt said, "Let's go to town." We went to town to a Japanese barber. They made me sit down

They would get wood from the sawmill, then go door to door selling it for firewood. At first they hauled the wood with a horse and buggy, but later they were able to buy their own trucks. Many Sikhs followed in the firewood business, which lasted until the 1950s.

Some of the immigrant Sikhs started their own lumber mills. Mayo and Kapoor Singh bought a failing lumber mill in New Westminster in 1914. In 1918 they started a larger mill near Duncan, on Vancouver Island. A small village grew up around the mill, which they called Paldi, after Mayo's hometown in India. Kapoor built another mill near Sooke Lake.

Sawmill crew and inspectors at the Sewall Mill on the Queen Charlotte Islands in the 1940s.

Life in Canada for most early Sikhs was connected with lumbering. In the 1920s some went to the small towns near Vancouver and to Kelowna and Kamloops to start farms. During the Depression, when many mills closed, Sikh workers went to farms to work during the harvest. When the economy improved, they returned to the mills.

The Sikh temple at 1866 West 2nd Avenue, Vancouver, around 1946. A European man is talking to the Sikh people.

and get a haircut. He said, "I don't want you to wear this turban around here." He then took me to buy some new clothes, thicker clothes for winter.

When immigrant groups come to Canada they feel they have to make some changes to fit in to the Canadian way of life. The individual as well as the new community has to decide what and how much of their culture they are willing to give up. Some believe they should change, while others want to keep the old country's ways. Conflicts between groups often result. The dominant society in Canada also has strong opinions about what and how much new immigrants should change.

The Sikh immigrants of the 1920s made concessions in order to fit in to their new life in Canada. They tried to fit in although the colour of their skin would always set them apart. Those who put aside their religious symbols felt that these were only surface changes—they had not given up their religion. They felt this was the price they had to pay for coming to this country and to make life easier.

Sikh workers at Royal City Mills near Vancouver around 1900–1910.

First at Bat in a New School

WHEN WORLD WAR II ENDED, IN AUGUST 1945, Ernest Hillen was eleven years old. He had spent the previous three and a half years in a Japanese prison camp in Indonesia. His father was Dutch and his mother Canadian. Ernest was born in Holland. When he was three, he moved with his family to Indonesia, a Dutch colony. During the war the Japanese took over the country and imprisoned the Europeans living there.

When Ernest left the prison camp, he walked, barefoot, through the barbed-wire gate, between his parents. He was carrying his friend Hubie's boots. Hubie had died in the camp and his mother had given Earnest the boots. The English guard at the gate gave them a salute. A passing jeep driven by a Sikh soldier gave the family a ride.

The Hillen family was free but Indonesia was still not a safe place. Mr. Hillen had to stay because of his job, but he felt that the others should leave. Indonesia was too dangerous, it was too expensive, and there were no proper schools. He wanted a normal life for Ernest and his elder brother, Jerry. He decided they should go to "*een land van melk en honing,*" a land of milk and honey, Canada.

Ernest, his mother, and his brother joined the postwar immigration wave—the largest immigration wave in history. People in many countries had lost their homes and belongings in the war and had nowhere to go. They began looking for a new place to live, for security, and for peace. Ernest, like many others, looked to Canada, and for the promise of Canada.

Ernest came to live in Toronto with his grandparents. He, like other newcomers to Canada, had to adapt to a new language and a new way of life, to billboards, snow, Campbell's soup, and baseball. It was an adventure. Most of all Ernest wanted to fit in, to be ordinary. His past was of no use here; his past was best forgotten. Here he recalls his first experiences at school in an excerpt from his book *Small Mercies: A Boy After War.*

Netherlands Ambassador Dr. J. H. van Roijin and Mrs. van Roijin greet Dutch immigrants as their ship docks in Montreal in 1947.

The first day of school, the third in Toronto, was amazing. The school yard was already filled with hundreds of running, shrieking children . . . Eyes down, I

marched through them in the short-pants English-boy suit and Hubie's extra-polished riding boots—my best outfit . . . Wide wooden stairs worn to a slope in the center, not so clean—and then the smell hit me. Ink, glue, carbolic soap, wood, paint, dust, running shoes. It was the smell of school.

In class Miss Tock didn't sit down. She pointed to the blackboard and then, smiling at me, said my name. In her clear way, she said Ernest had just arrived in Canada, and he was Dutch.

This was Ernest's first day in school, and lucky for them he'd be in their class! Welcome Ernest!

Welcome Ernest, the class muttered.

I felt two light pats on my back, like a "hello." I didn't turn around.

Miss Tock said the class was going to read now, and I could just sit and listen; next time I'd have my own book.

The bell rang. Books were tossed back inside the desks. Children rose. A hand on my shoulder turned me around: it was the patter.

C'mon! he said, and taking my elbow tugged me towards the door.

It's okay, the boy said. Recess.

The boy concentrated on slipping past those ahead, taking the stairs sometimes three at a time; I could do that.

Outside the Boys Entrance he stopped.

He was Ronald Glenesk, he said, squinting in the sudden bright daylight. What about baseball?

Yep, I said.

Had I played it?

Nope.

Had I seen it played?

Nope.

Never mind. C'mon!

One or two slapped me on the back. Friendly? Were they friendly slaps? They wore long pants, jackets with zippers, running shoes, and there was I in a pale-grey short-pants suit and riding boots. Oh God—I'd have to fight! All the dim days in camp, new boys had to

A BIRTHDAY LIST

Most of the people who became displaced after World War II had few belongings. The immigrants who came to Canada as refugees were in need. Their possessions had been taken from them or they had had no time to collect them before they fled.

When Ernest Hillen left prison camp, all he owned was a pair of shorts, a short-sleeved shirt, a harmonica, a backpack, a toy soldier, a beret, and Hubie's boots. His mother had only a skirt and shirt for working in, sandals, and a green dress. On the day they left the camp she wore the dress, which she had saved for that special day. The Hillen family had lost virtually all they owned before they went to the prison camp.

When the Hillens arrived in Canada there was still hardship, but soon after they arrived it was time to celebrate Ernest's birthday. Here is his birthday wish list, which his mother had suggested he write and pass around. The list, written in his newly acquired English, includes some items that suggest that Ernest had had a difficult past. See if you can figure out what he wanted.

Burth-list
a Dog
a Bibe gun with 500 bullets
a Stampablem
a Long pair of trouzes
a Jecked with a zipper
a very long and strong piese of rope with a sharp nife, PLEASE will you
a rugbiball
a bow and arrow's
a Expreswagon, with 4 wiels
a pair of boxgloves
a Pair of bedslippers
a baisebel secondhand
a pesket with al kainds of frood
6 tints with tomatejijce

fight, dizzy or not dizzy, sores or no sores—the rule of the tough; my rule, too.

Same team, Ernie! said a smiling Ronnie, suddenly beside me again. C'mon! and he jogged over to the corner of the yard's fence. Some boys quickly fanned out facing the corner; three of them busily scuffed up small mounds of cinders.

Someone handed him a bat. He passed it to me. I was First at Bat, he said, because I was the new guy. This was how I should grip it and swing it—and he showed me. The kid straight ahead holding the ball, he was the Pitcher. He'd throw the ball and I had to hit it and then run like hell to First Base. That was all for now. Three swings, okay?

Okay.

Ronnie joined a bunch of boys to the side, leaving me alone clutching the bat, except for a kid squatting behind me. I could feel a lot of eyes.

Play ball! Play ball! voices yelled.

I watched the Pitcher. A tall boy, he first twisted his body oddly and then threw the ball—but much too fast. I swung anyway, and almost fell over.

The squatter caught it though, and tossed it back to the Pitcher.

Nice swing, Ernie! Ronnie shouted. And others did, too—Nice swing, Ernie.

The Pitcher swivelled and threw the ball. Too fast again. I swung hard, but stayed on my feet. On whose side was the Pitcher?

Way to go, Ernie!

Way to go!

Nice try!

The squatter returned the ball. Whose side was he on?

This time the Pitcher swung himself half around and threw the ball—like a bullet. Not a ball that could be hit.

Strike three! somebody called. I laid the bat down.

Ernie received trousers, a zippered jacket, a beginner's stamp album, a twenty-foot-long piece of rope, a nine-inch-long knife in a leather sheath—and six cans of tomato juice. He was very happy.

Kimberley School in Toronto, which Ernie Hillen attended after arriving in Canada.

There was then some disagreement in Ronnie's group. Strange game: so far the only people who'd played were the Pitcher and me, and the squatter, I supposed. Everybody else, the boys fanned out in front and the ones to the side, just stood around. And then a voice from the side yelled: "Give ' im another chance!"

Another chance. Another chance. Some of the boys in front of me were then shouting it, too. Weren' t they the enemy?

Ronnie ambled over, grinning, and said I was still At Bat. I could try a few more hits.

The Pitcher then didn' t do his body trick, he just lobbed the ball over, and I almost hit it.

Atta boy, Ernie!

Atta boy!

The Pitcher tossed again, and I felt sure the bat touched the ball, though the ball didn' t change direction.

Close one, Ernie!

Close, close, close!

The next ball came at me like a kiss, in the sweetest, slowest way, just reaching for the bat — and I whacked it. It rolled in a fine straight line to the Pitcher.

And there was shouting! There was cheering. There was hand-clapping. The boy on First Base jumped up and down. I got the craziest feeling and clamped down my jaws. It was just as if I was going to cry.

Nice hit, Ernie!

Way to go!

Attaboy!

C' mon. Another one! . . .

When the lunch bell rang I ran home fast. There was a lot to tell; my mother would have questions.

After lunch I walked upstairs and changed clothes. Clothes, my cousin had told me, were important. I'd seldom wear Hubie' s boots again, the English-school-boy suit never. I was making a decision pulling on slobby long pants. I was going to be like the boys at school, not different, not special. I'd been special. No more! The plantation, the camps, pain and death, the boat, London, all that was really of no use here. So forget it. Start over. Become unspecial — fast.

In school, by the fourth day, the watch-and-listen plan was in full operation . . . it was what kids said and did that was important — everyday language, opinions, and jokes; gestures, postures, and faces pulled; ways of teasing, praising, and insulting. Kids were the teachers and one day I wanted it to show in their eyes that I was just one of them, no different.

Ernie learned to be ordinary. He left his past behind. He learned what to wear, how to talk, and to do push-ups. He got a job after school, went to his first dance, and was introduced to jazz. He decided he was going to be a lumberjack, trapper, or maybe a cowboy or a crooner. In the summer he worked at Rice Lake at a fishing lodge, where he spent his spare time painting rowboats.

A few years later Ernie returned to Indonesia. When he left the shores of North America an ache suddenly flared in him and stayed with him for the next few years. He had become ordinary—he had become a Canadian. And what good, he asked himself, was the "ordinary" in Indonesia? He remembered the summers at Rice Lake. "There wasn't anything I could compare painting rowboats to. It wasn't play. It wasn't work. What could be finer than painting rowboats in the sun? Sun burning, wind cooling, lake lapping, birds singing, thoughts roaming. There were moments when I felt I understood everything."

Ernie missed Canada. It was not, he said, a yearning for certain people or places, it was the promise of Canada. Ernie immigrated permanently to Canada when he turned eighteen in 1952.

LETTER TO A FRIEND

JANE ENG AND HER PARENTS IMMIGRATED TO Canada from Hong Kong in 1994. Hong Kong, a small area on the coast of China, used to be a British colony. In 1997, control over this territory was handed back to China. In the years leading up to 1997, many of the Chinese people in Hong Kong were worried about the future. They feared they would lose freedoms and opportunities. One incident especially frightened people. In 1989, in Tiananmen Square, in Beijing, China, many students were killed during a public demonstration. Chinese rule frightened Hong Kong residents and they wanted to leave before the 1997 handover. Jane and her family, and many others, came to Vancouver, British Columbia.

Jane had to adjust to her new country. She dreaded going to a new school. On the first day, she sat alone in a park next to the school and wrote a letter to her good friend, Cindy, back home. She told Cindy how she felt and of the many differences that frightened her—differences in language, school, clothing, and attitudes. Although Jane understood that the family had to leave Hong Kong, she hadn't wanted to go. She was angry and sad to leave her friends and everything that was familiar. She felt very alone and confused about where she fit in. Also, her father was going to go back to Hong Kong to work, and would be leaving her and her mother alone in the new land. Jane read this letter during a radio interview.

Dear Cindy,

I miss you so much. I'm sitting on a tree stump in a park next to my school. A place I come to think, to read and to escape. Well, anyway, let me tell you what happened today. This was a day I've been dreading ever since I got here—the first day of school. It was like I was in a zoo.

OK, imagine this—rows of lockers lining the hallways, kind of like those you see on TV actually. The colours in the school were so bad. The walls on one side were orange and on the other side they were light green. You just think of that—it's so mainland Chinesey. And all the people—they're everywhere swearing, girls with makeup on, not like us back home with our hair tied up nice and tidy in a ponytail. I wore mine like that today. It was weird. For the first time I felt like taking it down. I know we always thought those girls who wore their hair down were flirts, but today I didn't really feel that way.

Hong Kong's spectacular harbour and modern buildings dominate the city's skyline.

Chinese Canadians celebrate Halloween in Richmond, British Columbia, which has a large Asian population.

Oh, Cindy, it's not that I don't like this place, it's just so different. Boys and girls everywhere speaking English. There's so much I don't understand. How do I act around them, what do I say? I don't even know what to wear to school.

You know, Cindy, for me, it doesn't really matter that I look Chinese, though, there are lots of Chinese people here. What matters is how I feel inside. I felt so out of place. I didn't want to sit alone but everyone had their own friends. Nobody cared about me. I ended up sitting in front of my locker eating a sandwich by myself. I felt like such a loser.

The only thing that is familiar to me besides my family is my flute. When I play it all my fears seem to just slip away. I can forget at least for a little while that I'm here. When I left home I was just dying to

ASTRONAUT FAMILIES

Many immigrant families from Hong Kong experience a split in the family. The father gets the family settled in Canada but then returns to Hong Kong to work. Many fathers travel back and forth between Hong Kong and Canada, creating what are known as astronaut families. Here recent immigrants Jane, Andrea, and Brian share their thoughts about their astronaut families.

Jane (whose father is away for two months and home for one month): *The astronaut syndrome is not a 100 percent bad thing. Because in many cases, I heard, the relationship between sons and daughters and the father or the parents has improved. You learn not to take the family for granted. Then you want to cherish the times together and . . . you know how important the family can be to you. Every situation has a bad and good side. The family is not a sure thing.*

Andrea (whose father is away for three months and home for a few weeks): *I can see how much families can break apart and how important it is for my mom to have my dad here. It's just not complete when you have your dad in Hong Kong. If I had the choice I'd stay here and maintain a close relationship with my kids. I've been lucky enough to learn as much English as I have in Hong Kong that I can communicate without problems in Canada. I've been lucky to be able to adapt to this life so quickly. If you have the chance, really try to communicate more with people living here.*

Brian (whose father is away for six months and home for six months; his mother lives in Hong Kong): *I live with my sister and we have to depend on each other. We have to make our own dinner, do all the housework, take care of the finances, and take care of ourselves. My sister is seventeen years old. I have a lot of freedom. I can do what I want to do here. I can watch TV for three to four hours. If I want to go out I can go out anytime I want—I don't have to talk to my parents.*

The changeover ceremony on July 1, 1997, marking the transition from Hong Kong's association with the United Kingdom to its new status as a region of the People's Republic of China.

figure out who I was, now I'm just not so sure. I feel like my flute is the only piece of me that I have to grab on to. It reminds me of home. It's the only way I can really express myself these days.

I'm so confused, Cin. I don't know what kind of people I want to be with, or even know what I am going to be — Canadian or Chinese. Maybe I'll just stick with people from Hong Kong. They call them Hongers here. It's the easy way. But sometimes I think if I'm here in Canada now, why not reach out and explore more. Maybe I'll find a place where I really belong. It's funny. I haven't cried yet. It's strange I don't really feel anything. Remember how I cried every day when I was getting ready to leave? How I wrote the word Canada on a big piece of paper and tore it up into lit-

tle pieces? Maybe I used up all my tears before I came.

And I have to try to put on a smile for my parents. It took so much to get us in. I still don't really know why I'm here though. Sure I know with the takeover in '97 that we had to get out. But I feel betrayed sometimes. They always said we would stay through '97 but I guess Tiananmen changed their minds. Anyway, I know if I was stuck at home I wouldn't be happy either. Almost everyone's gone. Carmine is in Australia, Irene's in the States. You're the only one left, Cindy. Well I guess I'll have to stop here. My dad's van is just around the corner. He's flying back home next week and won't come back till Christmas. It's going to be just my mom and me. Oh, Cindy, I don't want to imagine how that will be. But I'm sure it will just turn out fine. Anyway, gotta go. Write back soon.

Love and hugs,
Jane

Jane made friends and became part of Vancouver's large Chinese community. She could speak Chinese, eat and shop in Chinese surroundings, and go to Chinese movies. It was not so different from her life in Hong Kong. But Jane found that not all Chinese Canadians were the same, and that she had a choice in deciding to become Chinese-Canadian. There were the new immigrants from Hong Kong, like herself, called Hongers, the Chinese who had their own culture. There were the Canadian-born, called CBCs, the Chinese who sometimes saw the whole Chinese culture and sometimes just a part of it. There were the bananas, the Chinese who wanted only to be Caucasian.

Jane also wanted to join the larger Canadian community. She understood that she was now in a different country and had a chance to make new friends. But she knew the two worlds were very different. Sometimes, going between the two worlds, she felt she had two faces. She felt like an actress figuring out which role to play. She solved her problem when she realized that she didn't have to worry about what she was. She decided just to be herself—Jane.

A Chinese float during Canada Day celebrations July 1, 2000 in Richmond, British Columbia.

THREE

Finding an Identity

Canadian immigrants have an ancestral heritage as well as a new Canadian culture. Having two cultures means that finding one's identity is not an easy task. In this chapter, Arvo, Cheryl, Gabrielle, and Muryl tell their stories about searching for, and finding, their identity.

Arvo tells how Canada became a place to create a new identity. Arvo and the people he was with had a dream about a new and ideal way of living. Cheryl tells how she tried to hide her origins to fit in. Eventually she found the courage to be proud of her heritage and her identity. Gabrielle describes how she felt when she went from her culture into the culture that was dominant in Canada. She was secure in her family ways, but very unsure of herself in the larger culture. Muryl tells how she lost her family heritage. She knew nothing of her ancestors. Her story describes the discovery of her roots and how this new information gave her a new identity.

These stories illustrate how important heritage is to identity. Immigrants joining the larger Canadian culture often look to the past, to their ancestors, in their search for identity. Learning about their heritage helps them understand who they are. These stories also show us that Canada is a place where one is able not only to learn from the past but to create a new society. Coming to Canada gives many people a chance for a better and different life. People can find their individual identities by learning about, accepting, and preserving their heritage, and by dreaming of the ideal community.

With so many people from different countries in Canada, marriages between people from different countries are common. After a few generations of intermarriage, one's ancestral heritage becomes more and more complex. Finding an identity in such cases can be difficult. The following poem expresses one person's feelings about his mixed heritage and what it means to him to be Canadian.

MY GENEALOGY

John Robert Colombo

1.
My great-great-grandfather
played in the streets
of Milano, I am told.
I take it on faith.

2.
His son, the artisan,
immigrated to Baden, Ontario,
as a decorator or builder.
I believe this, but never met him.

3.
My grandfather was born
in Baden, and he married
a German girl there.
I remember him well—
he spoke English
with a German accent.

4.
My grandparents lived
in Berlin, Ontario,
when it changed its name
to honour Lord Kitchener.
They made an unusual couple—
he was more than six feet tall,
she barely five—but together
they produced fourteen children.

5.
One of these fourteen Colombos
was my father. He spoke English
with a Pennsylvania-Dutch accent.

6.
He married a Kitchener girl,
and I was born in that city—
with its light industry
and its farmer's market—
in that city, an only child.

7.
I remember quite distinctly
my mother's parents, my grand-
parents. My grandfather spoke
with a thick Greek accent,
and my larger grandmother,
a nasal Quebec French. Yes,
they made a colourful couple.

8.
They first met in Montreal,
lived in Toronto for a while,
finally settled in Kitchener.
They had five children,
and their arguments had to be
heard to be believed.

9.
Blood flows through my veins
at different speeds:
Italian, German,
Greek, French-Canadian.
Sometimes it mixes.

10.
At times I feel close
to the Aegean,
the Cote d' Azure,
the Lombard Plain,
and the Black Forest.

11.
I seldom feel close
to the Rocky Mountains,
the Prairies,
the Great Lakes,
or the cold St. Lawrence.
What am I doing in Toronto?

12.
If this means being Canadian,
I am Canadian.

SOINTULA: DREAMS OF UTOPIA

ON DECEMBER 6, 1901, FIVE FINNISH IMMIGRANTS from Nanaimo, British Columbia, boarded a five-and-a-half-metre sailboat, the *Aino*. They were going on a 290-kilometre journey north. Their destination was Malcolm Island, a small island between the B.C. mainland and Vancouver Island. These Finns, and the others who followed them, were looking for a "promised land."

The Finns had found working in the coal mines of Nanaimo dreadful. It was exhausting and dangerous. The living quarters were rough shacks. The social life was the tavern. The mine owner did nothing to improve the situation.

The Finns dreamed of creating a utopia, an ideal community where people would live in harmony. They invited a Finn named Matti Kurikka to lead them. Kurikka

was an outspoken idealist who had already tried to build a utopian community in Australia. The Finns gave their new home the name Sointula, which means harmony in Finnish. Kurikka described the Finns' vision for Sointula this way:

We will be self-sufficient and produce everything we need. Unemployment and sickness will evaporate into the past and strikes and poverty will become unknown . . . Only then will the characteristics of our nationality have an opportunity to blossom and prosper.

A group of Finnish settlers on Malcolm Island, near Vancouver Island, in 1919.

Throughout history people have tried to build utopian communities. Sointula was meant to be such a community, built on love, freedom, equality, and harmony between people and nature. It would give the Finnish immigrants a new life and a new identity. The idea of a utopia appealed to many Finns. Men, women, and children began landing on the shores of the forested island. The newcomers were of all trades—farmers, doctors, shoemakers, and miners. Some came directly from Finland. Others were recent immigrants who had settled in Canada and the United States.

Arvo Tynjala was six when he came to Sointula. His father had come from Finland in 1890 and had settled on a farm in North Dakota. But in the following decade there was a depression and crops were poor. His father had heard that there was fertile farmland on Sointula and decided to go there. The Tynjalas and four other families headed north in a caravan of wagons, with plows, livestock, and a piano.

In 1967, many decades after settling in Sointula, Arvo was interviewed about the community and what it was like to live there. Here is an excerpt from the interview.

What were the aims and ideals of this movement? What were they trying to do?
Times were hard in those days and the people were working for low wages at the mines in Nanaimo. They started to think of some better possibilities than working in the mine for nothing. They got together and they started dreaming about this thing, that it could be an easier and better way of making a living.

What is the thing that they were dreaming about?
The community effort. To live in a co-operative community instead of individually. They would go together like a big family and live together.

Did they own everything in common?
Yes. That was the understanding. That's how they got

THE *AIKA*, A COMMUNITY NEWSPAPER

Many ethnic groups in Canada have their own newspapers. Through their newspapers, immigrants communicate with people from their own country, in their own language, and find out what others are doing in communities across the country.

The Finnish miners had their own handwritten newspaper when they were in Nanaimo. The miners used the paper to express their concerns about their working conditions. They also wrote about their hopes for a new community. The newspaper helped begin the plans for moving to Sointula.

When Matti Kurikka arrived in Nanaimo, the miners decided to start a printed newspaper. They bought an old printing press from an English newspaper company. A Finnish newspaper firm in New York donated Finnish type. They named the newspaper the *Aika*, which means "the Times." It started on May 6, 1901, the first printed Finnish newspaper in Canada.

The *Aika* became a weekly paper, with subscribers in Finnish settlements in Canada, the United States, and Finland. It carried news items from North America and Finland, as well as poems, stories, proverbs, riddles, and advertisements. One of the main features was Kurikka's writing. His articles explained and promoted the utopian community of Sointula. In the first issue of the newspaper, his article "The Harmony Idea" encouraged people to come to the planned community.

Come here to live with us in freedom, where all are equal in the harmony of shared thoughts, and all find satisfaction and pleasure in

this island from the government. They would own the whole island.

How were they going to make their living?
There were different possibilities. There was logging—the whole island was covered with good timber. Fishing—the same as we have been doing ever since. But I think they had big plans. Lots of them were coming from farms, and farming was their idea . . . They counted quite a bit on farming, not realizing that it was heavy timber growing all over the island, that it wasn' t so easy to get the farmland cleared.

Was the idea, too, that they would . . . be as self-sustaining as possible?
Yes. I think that was the understanding, because they had the shoemakers and tailors and doctors and everything else in their own group.

Even doctors?
There was at least one certified doctor, and possibly two.

Did they have schoolteachers?
It was a kind of kindergarten system, but it lasted only a short time. The government had to take over.

Were there many children in the first years of the community?
There were quite a few children, but mostly small children at the time [the island community was established]. There were some older kids.

But it was mostly young families, I suppose.
Yes, most of them were in their thirties, and, of course, lots of them younger than that.

They were all young and idealistic people.
Yes.

Could you describe what activity was going on around there then?
The people went to work. They built the sawmill first. Then they started sawing lumber for their own use here. That's why the apartment house that I

---

the protection of the weak.
Bring your entire effects . . . people are needed who are congenial, unselfish, devoted, and willing to sacrifice much.

When the Finns from Nanaimo moved to Sointula, they brought the printing press with them. They started the *Aika* again in November 1903. Every two weeks 1,500 copies were printed. The *Aika* carried news of Sointula and described it as a thriving community, but only fourteen issues were printed before the community broke up. By December 1904 publication of the *Aika* had stopped.

The front page of the Aika, *a Finnish newspaper in British Columbia in 1901.*

The wharf at Sointula in the early 1900s.

mentioned was delayed. They had to get the sawmill working.

How was the community house to work? Was anybody to live in individual houses?
It was just like an apartment house, only they had a community cookhouse. They had an eating mess house—a big one with long tables. Generally, people would go to the cookhouse to eat. The apartment house was only for sleeping quarters.

People kept coming to Sointula. By the end of 1902, more than two hundred people lived in the community. An apartment building, sawmill, library, pier, and nursery were built according to plan. The people were enthusiastic and willing to work hard.

The utopian community, however, did not last long. The dream failed for many reasons. The settlers were most-ly professionals or artisans and knew little of the work that needed to be done. In 1903 a fire burned down the apartment building and eleven people died. Quarrels began about certain ideas for the community. Matti Kurikka had little business knowledge and debts grew.

In 1904, Kurikka left, with about half the settlers. The last meeting of the community took place on May 27, 1905. The utopian society had collapsed, but it was not a complete failure. About a hundred people stayed on. They made a fresh start. To make a living, many went to work in logging and fishing. Arvo's family stayed in Sointula. Arvo got a job as a boat puller when he was fourteen.

The Finns were not the first group to try to create a utopia on Malcolm Island, nor would they be the last. In the 1960s, hippies joined the Finns to look for their own utopia. There are now more than seven hundred people living on the island.

HAIRDAY: PRESSING IDENTITY INTO SUBMISSION

CHERYL FOGGO WAS BORN AND GREW UP IN Calgary in the 1960s. She is a fourth-generation Canadian. In 1910, her great-grandparents came to Canada. They were Black immigrants from the United States.

Cheryl's relatives were part of a huge immigration wave to Canada. After the Canadian Pacific Railway was completed, the Canadian government encouraged people to come and settle the West. Many immigrants came from Europe, but many also came from the United States. Between 1905 and 1912, nearly two thousand Black men, women, and children came to settle in the plains of western Canada. Many of these settlers had been successful farmers in Oklahoma, and they prospered in Canada.

The Black Americans assumed they would be welcomed. But the times and circumstances of the early 1900s made the immigration of the Black settlers difficult. White settlers resisted the newcomers, and in 1911 the govern-ment discussed passing laws to stop Black immigration. The laws were not passed, but entering the country became very difficult for Black people.

Many groups who come to Canada have problems deciding where they belong—in their original groups or in Canadian society. The pressures they feel often depend on the size of their group. The Blacks in the West felt a great deal of pressure because there were so few of them. As they moved to the cities to work in the 1930s and 1940s, they became even more isolated in the White community and from other Blacks. This was a problem Cheryl faced. She was an isolated Black child in a predominantly White society.

Cheryl Foggo tells of her many experiences growing up in this environment in her book *Pourin' Down Rain.* This excerpt from the book describes how she, her sister, and their mother changed their appearance. They straight-

Cheryl and her siblings after a "hairday." From left: Richard, Noël , Cheryl, and Ronny.

ened their hair to comply with the dominant view of beauty in Canada.

Hairday, as my sister and I referred to it, was a torment, a day of relentless brushing, pulling, plunging into the yellow tub of water and then, at the end, the dreaded "hot comb." After a vigorous towel-drying at the hands of our mother, there was an hour's grace for air-drying, then we endured another hour, longer for me because of my thicker (bad) hair, beside the gas stove. We were stationed in a kitchen chair, eye-level with the blue flame that licked and scorched the heavy, iron pressing comb. Our mother divided our hair into tiny strands, coated each strand with Vaseline (wealthier Black people than we ordered products they called brilliantine from the U.S. for this purpose), then applied the teeth of the comb from our scalps to the ends of our hair. We felt the heat, heard the sizzle, smelled the burning protein and saw the smoke rise into the air around us.

As torturous as hairday was for Noël and me, it must have been triply so for my mother. By the end of the day spent wrestling with our hair and her own, she was always exhausted. Enduring my wailing atop everything else was clearly too much for her. It was a bit of genius on her part to tell me one evening that the next day was hairday, but that my friend Mary would also be coming to spend the day.

Her purpose in dropping both bits of news at the same time was to distract me from the unpleasantness of hairday. She wished to avoid the arguing and the protests that I would normally have presented . . .

The next morning, just before my mother plunged my head into the yellow tub, she looked at Mary, who was sitting, smiling, in a chair near the door. "I'll bet you don't cry when you get your hair done, do you Mary?" she said.

"No," Mary said, still grinning.

I, of course, shed nary a tear that hairday, nor at any other in the future.

AN AFRICAN ANCESTOR

Cheryl Foggo began to understand something about where she came from by studying Black culture and history. She was told the story of her ancestors. She learned about her family's trials and triumphs on their farm on the Prairies and about the problems they had before they came to Canada. She became proud of her heritage and who she was. She discovered that the real story of the Black people was different from the identity given them by White society. She discovered how one of her ancestors came from Africa to America. His name was Kudjo. Here is Kudjo's story, as told by Cheryl's Aunt Daisy.

In the early nineteenth century, an African named Kudjo lived near the Nile River in Ethiopia with his wife and three children. One morning Kudjo noticed some White men. They were unloading some cargo from a large ship. Keeping a safe distance, he watched them for some time before he returned home. He told his wife all that he had seen.

Kudjo was curious about these strangers. Over the next few days he kept going back to where the ship was docked to see what they were doing. He gradually lost his fear of the men and decided to approach them. They immediately befriended him. The strangers gave him gifts for himself and his family.

For the next few weeks, Kudjo went to visit his new friends every day. One day, the ship captain invited him and his family to a party that they were having that evening. His wife was alarmed with her husband's friendship with these strangers. She refused to go and begged him not to go. Kudjo

As for my mother, she achieved more than one goal. Added to her victory over my tears was the opportunity to "do" Mary's hair, a chance that she had been clearly waiting for.

I had once overheard her talking about Mary to one of her sisters. "I don't think Margaret knows what to do with her hair," she had said.

Mary, the accidental product of a biracial liaison, had been adopted into the family of one of my father's post office co-workers, Ray and his wife Margaret. They were a remarkable couple, both Caucasian, whose mostly adopted family of five included children who are usually hard to place—biracial, handicapped or older children. My mother admired them very much, but often fretted about Mary's hair, which she believed was a puzzle to her adoptive mother. By inviting Mary to visit us on hairday she not only conquered my tears, but Mary's hair as well, pressing it into sub-mission the way that she pressed my hair, my sister's and her own.

One day when Cheryl was fourteen, she decided that there would be no more hairdays. She would lay claim to her heritage. She went to school in an Afro hairstyle, which allowed her hair to curl naturally, showing that she was proud to be Black. Some classmates snickered as she walked into the classroom. One shouted, "Cheryl, did you stick your finger into an electrical outlet?" Her fellow students burst into laughter.

Cheryl had to decide who she was in the White world. She retreated from White culture and began to explore Black history and culture. She longed to belong to a larger Black world, but there were so few Blacks in her area. Eventually she understood that it was okay to be different. She found her identity. She explains it this way:

ignored his wife's warnings.

He went to the party and drank so much he became unconscious. When he woke up, he was at sea, far from his home and family. He would never see them again.

In America Kudjo became a slave. He repeatedly ran away until he was given a wife. He had three children. After the third child was born he started running away again. He wanted to be free. On one of his escapes he was sleeping in the branches of a tree. He was awakened by the barking of dogs. The dogs had tracked him. Kudjo was killed.

Some of the earliest settlers in Canada's West were Black people. Here an Indian agent in southern Alberta meets with some chiefs in 1886. The third man from the left in the back row, Dave Mills, was a half-Black interpreter.

Cheryl Foggo now lives in Calgary with her husband, Clem Martini. They have two children. Cheryl writes books and magazine articles.

It is difficult for someone who has never been different to understand. That one day that different child must tell herself that she has a right to exist. When you are a Black child who looks out into the world and sees hostility towards Blackness, you ask yourself why. One day you realize the hatred is not your fault. That day, you say, "I belong in the world. I belong here in Western Canada where my family has lived and worked for four generations."

Cheryl began to find her own identity by learning about her ancestors. She felt their sorrow, and discovered their pride and perseverance. She knew where she had come from and the strength of those before her.

CROSSING THE PROVENCHER BRIDGE

GABRIELLE ROY WAS BORN IN 1909 AND GREW UP in St. Boniface, Manitoba. This suburb of Winnipeg started out as, and remains, a French community. The people of St. Boniface speak French and have their own church, schools, and hospitals.

For Gabrielle, life was safe in the familiar surroundings of St. Boniface. However, she and her mother would go to Winnipeg to shop, and that meant going into another world. They would cross the Provencher Bridge over the Red River, which separates Winnipeg from St. Boniface.

In Winnipeg, the St. Boniface French people were foreigners. Winnipeg was made up of English and various other ethnic groups. Eaton's, the store at which Gabrielle and her mother shopped, was thought of as high class and English. It symbolized another world in which Gabrielle did not feel she belonged. She felt unsure of

The Provencher Bridge, built in 1918, still spans the Red River today, linking downtown Winnipeg to historic St. Boniface, seen here in the background.

THE ACADIANS: AN UPROOTED PEOPLE

In 1604, a group of eighty French settlers arrived in Acadia, which would later be called Nova Scotia, to start a new colony. In 1621, however, the land was granted to Sir William Alexander, a Scotsman. Both the English and the French populations grew. By 1750, there were between ten and fifteen thousand French and only two thousand English. Control of Acadia moved back and forth between the French and the English, but after 1713, it remained in the hands of the English.

Relations between England and France deteriorated, and the two countries were at war by the 1750s. The governor of Nova Scotia decided to rid Acadia of the French settlement. Deportation of the Acadians began in 1755. The English burnt the Acadians' farms and took their livestock. It is estimated that three-quarters of the Acadian population was deported.

Gabrielle Roy's ancestors were Acadians. From her mother, she learned that the struggle for the rights of the French had begun in the distant past. Here, Gabrielle recounts her mother's story about the Acadians.

"It all started," recounted Maman, "when the English stole our land — the farms we had back there in our first home, when we had one — because they saw how good it was there in the land of Evangeline. So they could get those rich farms for themselves, they rounded us up, put us on leaky ships, then took us far away and left us in places we'd never seen before."

"We are Acadians?"

"That's how our troubles began, a very long time ago," she said. "I don't know the whole story. Only bits, handed down from one generation to another."

herself, ashamed, and out of place in Winnipeg. This all changed when she crossed the bridge back into her neighbourhood. She would once again become secure and proud, overjoyed to be at home.

French Canadians, and many immigrant groups, have to cross a bridge from their own culture to the dominant Canadian culture. They live in two worlds, and this often causes a crisis in identity. Gabrielle Roy tells of her life in St. Boniface in her autobiography, *Enchantment and Sorrow*. In this excerpt, she describes what crossing the Provencher Bridge meant to her.

We almost always set off in high spirits and full of expectation. Maman would have read in the paper or heard from a neighbour that Eaton's was having a sale of curtain-lace, or printed cottons suitable for making aprons or house-dresses, or maybe children's shoes. As we left Maman was most often bubbling with merriment. So when we crossed the bridge, we were rich, with all our possible acquisitions still intact in our heads.

But as soon as we were on the other side, we'd undergo a kind of transformation that made us draw together, as though solidarity would help us face a kind of shadow that had fallen over us. It was partly because we were now on dismal Water Street beside the railway sorting yards. But there was more to it than that. Our discomfort came partly from inside us too. We'd suddenly be less sure of ourselves.

We'd arrive at Portage Avenue. We'd still be speaking French, of course, but perhaps less audibly, particularly after two or three passersby turned around and stared at us. The humiliation of having someone turn to stare when I was speaking French in a Winnipeg street was something I'd felt so often as a child that I no longer realized it was humiliation. Besides, I'd often turned around myself to stare at some immigrant whose soft Slavic voice or Scandinavian accent I'd heard. I got so used to it eventually that I suppose I thought of it as natural for us all to feel more or less like foreigners on someone else's ground.

A painting of Acadian farmers repairing a dyke in Nova Scotia.

together in Connecticut. They used to work in factories, in the bush, and on the railways, wherever there was hard work to be done cheap. But they looked out for each other, and were a comfort to each other in their homesickness.

"In those days," she said, "there were priests called colonizers, whose whole lives you'd swear depended on finding lost flocks and bringing home as many sheep as possible. One of them came to us in Connecticut. Some [Acadians] stayed, so we ought to

"Where were we taken to, Maman?"

"Oh, here and there in America. They didn't even know the *language where they ended up. They had to get along however they could. With great difficulty, one group managed to get back*

Only when we arrived at Eaton's was it decided whether or not there would be a confrontation. It all depended on Maman's frame of mind. Sometimes she'd begin by calling for a saleswoman who spoke our language to serve us. In our patriotic moments, we of St. Boniface claimed it was our right and even our duty to make a point of doing so, and that if all of us did this, industry and department stores would be obliged to hire our people.

So if Maman was having one of her good days, if her confidence was up and her tongue felt nimble, she'd take the offensive and demand one of our compatriots to wait on us. The more forceful she was, I'd observed, the more accommodating the floorwalker would be. He'd lose no time sending for Miss or Mrs. So-and-so, who often turned out to be someone we knew, sometimes even a neighbour.

"Madame Roy!" the saleslady would exclaim. "How are you? What can I do for you? It's always such a pleasure to help you."

It seems to me we poor people of St. Boniface had

Portage Avenue in Winnipeg, looking east, in about 1928. Eaton's is the building on the right.

a gift for neighbourly warmth when thrown together, handed down from some gracious society of olden times.

On days like that we probably bought more than we should have, being so grateful to be doing it in our own language that the money slipped through our fingers even faster than usual.

have some distant cousins in Connecticut, and some came and settled in the lovely, fertile parish of St. Jacques l' Achigan."

"Why did you leave?" I asked.

"Your grandfather felt too hemmed in by those barren hills and wouldn't be able to settle his sons around him. Then another colonizing priest came our way, this time to tell us wonderful things about Manitoba and how we'd be made to feel at home here. He talked about the beautiful rich land and all the Canadian West where we should hurry to go and get established before the Scots and English, who were arriving in

droves in those days. He told us the whole country from ocean to ocean belonged to us, we of French blood, because of the French explorers who'd been all over it first. Our rights to our language and our religion would be respected. Our family was on the move again. They were granted land in the Pembina Mountain settlements.

"After a few years everything could have been wonderful at St. Leon because the land was ours. Then the Manitoba government turned against us. It passed that dreadful law forbidding French to be taught in our schools. We were trapped, far away from our second

home. We couldn't afford to leave, and besides, where would we have gone?"

"So we were without a home again?" I asked.

"We still had our land, our customs, our houses, and our language, but that's what ruined us too—that long struggle, and all the money we had to spend to keep our schools."

For Gabrielle Roy, knowing where her family had come from gave her pride in her culture and heritage. It also helped her to find her own place in Canadian society.

But there were also times when Maman felt beaten before she began, weary of a struggle that had to be taken up again and again and was never won for good and all. At such times she found it simpler and less taxing to "bring out" her English, as she used to say.

We'd move from counter to counter. Using her hands and facial expressions to help, she really managed pretty well, though sometimes a real problem arose, like the time she wanted some chamois ("shammy" to the English) to line a coat, and asked for "a yard or two of Chinese skin to put under the coat."

When a saleswoman failed to understand her, she would call another to help, and sometimes that one would call a third. Passing customers would stop to help too, for Winnipeg, while it treated us as foreigners, was nothing if not quick to fly to our assistance the moment we found ourselves in a fix. To us these incidents were pure torture. Sometimes we'd slip away in the middle of it all. Then we'd be overcome with mirth at the thought of all those good-hearted folk no doubt still arguing over how to rescue us, with us already far from the scene . . .

We came home from our expeditions to Winnipeg dog-tired and, in truth, almost always depressed. Though we crossed the bridge on the way out with

Taken about 1925, this photo shows young Gabrielle Roy on the right, her sister Bernadette in the middle, and their mother on the left.

our heads full of plans as if we were rich, we never recrossed it feeling anything but poor . . . There were times, once we were back in our own city, when [Maman would] look up at the tall sky with a kind of rapture. Often the weariness would vanish from her face as if by magic and she'd declare, as if calling me to witness: "It's good to be home!"

Gabrielle Roy began to create her own identity as a young girl. She began to understand what St. Boniface meant to her and what it represented in the larger English society. Her trips to Winnipeg portrayed the feelings and struggles the French Canadians had had for many generations. They had wanted and tried to preserve their heritage. They felt uncomfortable in the larger Canadian society.

Gabrielle Roy grew up to become one of Canada's most famous authors. She taught in Manitoba and lived in England and France, studying drama. Her books are celebrated not only by the French, but by all Canadians. Through her writings, Gabrielle continued to struggle for the French. The struggle became part of her identity.

The Roy family home on rue Deschambault in St. Boniface, Manitoba, around 1910.

HERITAGE LOST AND FOUND

All immigrants have their own unique story about how and why they came to Canada. The stories as told in pictures, documents, and family trees are passed from one generation to the next. These family histories become part of the identity of the members of each family. But not all Canadians are so lucky as to have such an identity. Some people know very little and some know next to nothing about their heritage.

There are various reasons why some Canadians have no family history. Many orphaned children were brought to Canada throughout the 1900s. They would likely have no knowledge about their relatives. As well, many children became orphans after their families arrived in Canada. Many lost all contact with relatives and would not even know their ethnic origin. Other people simply lost their heritage little by little over the generations.

Many Canadians want to know more about their family roots. They begin to search for information about their ancestors. They try to find lost relatives in Canada and other countries. They study their family history, a practice called genealogy. People can trace their ancestors in many ways. In libraries, for example, information can be found in ships' registers, birth and death records, homestead deeds, and histories of early pioneers.

Muryl Anderson was born in Winnipeg in the 1930s. When she was eleven, she moved with her family to B.C. Both her parents then lost contact with their relatives on the Prairies, so Muryl did not learn where her ancestors were from. Here, Muryl describes her journey to discover her family's identity. She recalls her confusion about her ethnic origin when she was a child. She then talks about her amazing adventures looking for her family roots. In the late 1980s, Muryl found out that her past lay in a country that she had never imagined she was from. At last, she was able to meet her relatives. At last, she could walk on the paths where her forefathers had walked. She wrote her story for this book.

WHAT'S IN A NAME?

Many immigrants change their first names and even their family names when they come to Canada. They do this to fit in and to lessen the difference between themselves and their new fellow citizens. In the past, changing a name was easy and often done informally. Muryl Anderson discovered that her grandfather changed his surname from Andrejciw to Anderson—in fact, he changed his name a total of twenty-three times.

Surnames very often denote a person's country of origin. A typical Ukrainian surname ending is -enko. Because the Ukraine has frequently been under Polish rule, Ukrainian names have much in common with Polish names. Many Ukrainian surnames end in -uk, which corresponds to the Polish ending, -ik. Some Ukrainian names come from patron saints of the Poles.

The name Andrejciw corresponds to the English name Andrew. Andrew was the first disciple of Jesus and a name known and used throughout Christian

Ukrainian immigrants Joe Wacha and his wife are plastering a house near Vita, Manitoba, in 1916.

regions. Andrew is a patron saint of Scotland and Russia, and a popular name in Poland and the Czech Republic. However, in each

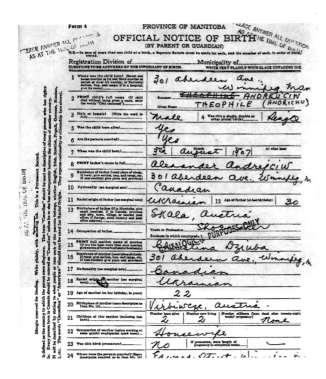

The birth certificate of Theophile Andrejciw, who became Philip Anderson, Muryl's father.

When I was a child in Winnipeg, I was just another Canadian kid. I spoke English at home to my parents, who also spoke English. At school we played softball and we skipped rope in the summer. In winter we threw snowballs and made snow angels lying down in the snow. Everyone was "Canadian."

Then a family questionnaire was given out by the school for our parents. The main question was: What is your ethnic origin? My mother was puzzled. She had been orphaned at five years of age and raised in a French-Canadian home. She had lost her ethnic origin. My father was working in a logging camp in British Columbia so she couldn't ask him. Finally, my mother put down Scandinavian. My father had once said his family was Scandinavian.

Next year she put down Danish. Another year it was Scottish, then English . . . I was becoming the United Nations, all by myself! Her confusion didn't bother me as I loved to read the series of books called Children of Other Lands. *This was the beginning of*

language the name appears in a slightly different form—Andrew in English, André in French, Drees in German, or Andrzej in Polish. Andrew is also a surname—Anderson in English, Andersen in Danish, or Andrzejak in Polish.

One culture often has difficulty pronouncing, spelling, or remembering the names found in another culture. For example, English people can have difficulty with Asian names. The Chinese have their own writing system, and their names do not correspond with English names. In a land registry in Victoria in the mid-1800s, the names of the owners of a certain property were first written as Chang Foon Hung, Chin Fong Hong, and Sou Kong Ho. Later, these names were crossed out and replaced with Chin Foon Hung, Chin Foon Hong, and Sou Kong Ho. Eventually, all the names were crossed out and replaced with the words "Owned by 3 Chinamen."

Chinese people, by the same token, can have a great deal of trouble with English names. For example, in the 1860s a restaurant owner named Lee Sing went to court because some of his patrons owed him money. Here is the list of patrons that Lee Sing submitted. No doubt the judge would have had great difficulty identifying the debtors.

Lean Man White Man	$20.00
French Old Man	$ 8.00
Get Tight Man	$ 7.50
Indian Joe	$10.00
Fat Frenchman	$30.62
Lame Leg Man	$40.00
Red Whiskers	$18.50
Captain of the Schooner	$50.00
Shoemaker Gone to California	$15.00
Red Shirt Man	$27.00

Names in another language can be a source of embarrassment for immigrants wanting to fit in to a larger culture. However, as a link to the past, they can also be a source of cultural pride.

my wanting to have an ethnic heritage, to "be part of something," to "belong," like my school friends.

When I had finished school and earned some money, I left Vancouver with my ten-speed bike to travel the world. I went to Scandinavia and worked and lived in Denmark. I travelled around Europe and then set off for Asia—by bike, hitchhiking, donkey rides, and airplane. I was gone ten years. I came back to Canada still with a need to find out who I was. I loved travelling and I wanted to walk the same roads where my ancestors once walked.

I began to search for my family roots—I became a family "Private Eye." I had no idea of the next great adventure that was in store for me. I sent for documents—birth, marriage, and death registrations and homestead records. What a surprise! I wasn't Scandinavian, English, or Scottish! I was Ukrainian! Both my parents were of Ukrainian origin. My mother's name wasn't Normand, but Sawczuk! My father's name wasn't Anderson, but Andrejciw!

Next, I spent hours in libraries reading stories about early Ukrainian pioneers. One day when I was in the genealogy section of the library, I found a book that gave a full record of the arrival of my mother's family in Canada. "I don't believe it!" I shouted out. The librarian and people around me looked up. Everyone was smiling. They hoped they too would one day make an exciting discovery about their lost families.

When I discovered I had Ukrainian roots, I was at first overjoyed. Then I was depressed. I thought about all of those lost years when I could have learned the Ukrainian language and about the culture, been part of a Ukrainian community in Canada, and maybe even learned how to do Ukrainian dancing. In a way, I felt I had been robbed.

Suddenly I became a born-again Ukrainian! I became more Ukrainian than Ukrainians in Ukraine. I took language courses, became director of a Ukrainian cultural centre, and had an exhibit in Canada's

Muryl Andrejciw Anderson (left) and Janice Harnishyn Horne in Hutsul wedding costumes from the Carpathian Mountains in Ukraine where Muryl's maternal grandmother was born and raised.

National Ukrainian Festival in Dauphin, Manitoba. I loved to wear a Ukrainian blouse.

I decided to go with a tour group to Ukraine to visit my grandparents' villages. I wrote each ancestral village and told them my date of arrival and all the information about my grandparents. I was told I would never get an answer. Three months later when I was leaving, there was still no reply.

It was thrilling when our airplane landed near Kiev, the capital city of Ukraine. Our tour took us from Kiev to the Black Sea, and on to the province where my father's parents were from. The train stopped in the city of Ternopil. Someone from our tour group leaped out, as he was expecting relatives to meet him. He was surrounded and hugged by a group of people with armloads of flowers. The rest of us looked on enviously.

Suddenly our friend turned and got back on the train. "Muryl," he exclaimed, "these people aren' t my relatives. They' re yours! They have the letter you wrote." He pushed me into the arms of the crowd with the letter and I could hear them calling, "Miril, Miril, Miril."

I went into shock. I couldn' t remember one word of Ukrainian that I had learned. I started to cry, and then the whole group was crying. Overwhelmed, I looked into the faces of these complete strangers who were now my family.

I learned that these people were from my grandmother's and grandfather's villages. For the next five days they followed our tour bus wherever it went. I learned that a smile and hug say everything that words can say when you can' t speak the language.

That day was only a beginning. I made four trips to Ukraine to get to know my new relatives. One of those trips was to my mother's village in the Carpathian Mountains.

I had completed my journey of discovery. I now knew who I was. The pieces of the puzzle were put snugly in their rightful places. I felt a peace that I had never had before in my life. After ninety years, I had reconnected our family.

I no longer felt I had to be more Ukrainian than the Ukrainians. I had been Canadian, Ukrainian, Ukrainian-Canadian, Canadian-Ukrainian, and finally I was back to being—Canadian.

Muryl worked very hard to find her family roots. The discovery of her Ukrainian background and her travels to meet her relatives gave her an identity that had been missing. Many people search for years and years to know something about their relatives who first came to the adopted country. Many never find them, but many others are successful. One never knows what one will discover in these searches. One might uncover an ethnic or religious background that was lost or hidden, or ancestors who were pirates, great warlords, or carpenters. The surprises make the exploration an exciting adventure.

Muryl now lives in Vancouver with her husband. She is content that she has found out about her real past, but she hasn't given up her private eye adventures. She continues to be involved in genealogy, helping others find their heritage. She gives lectures and has written a resource book, *Finding Your Ukrainian Ancestors.*

Muryl is seen here welcoming people of Ukrainian heritage to her Village Registry, where she traced the ancestral villages that immigrants came from.

FOUR

Discrimination and Prejudice

Many immigrants find a better life in Canada, free from persecution or death. By immigrating, they hope for a more promising life for themselves and their children. Some, however, face discrimination and prejudice. The history of Canadian immigration has not been perfect. Canadian society has not always accepted newcomers. It has acted against those who were different, sometimes subtly and sometimes aggressively. At times the immigrants faced discrimination as soon as they arrived; at other times, discrimination surfaced only after many years. In this chapter, some of the negative sides of immigration are told in stories of Mary, Lara, and Chu.

One way to deal with individuals or groups who are not wanted in a society is to keep them separate. The most severe method that can be used is to physically confine them. During World Wars I and II, the Canadian government relocated many Canadians who originated from countries that were, during the wars, enemy countries. During World War II, Japanese Canadians were interned. In this chapter, Mary tells what happened to her Japanese-Canadian family.

People who are seen as different can be pushed away, or they can be forced to change. Lara was different because of her religious beliefs, and these beliefs conflicted with some of the basic ideas of the dominant culture. She was taken from her family and put in a school to become an "Englishwoman." Lara talks about her time at school and the hardships she endured.

Limiting a group's access to jobs, schools, where they can live, where they are buried—the basic freedoms the rest of society enjoys—is another way to keep people who are different away. Some immigrants were restricted by the limits placed on them. Paul Yee's story about Chu, a son searching for his father who had disappeared after he came to Canada, addresses the hardships endured by early Chinese immigrants who could not bring their families.

These stories reveal some ways that discrimination and prejudices have marked our history. These are not three isolated examples; they represent other groups and individuals who have suffered injustices at certain times in their lives or on a daily basis. The tales are a sad part of our history. They are tales of a lack of understanding and of a passion for one's own way, above the rights and freedoms of others.

To keep a group separate, restrictions can be placed on how people travel. Although transportation has not been segregated in Canada as in some other countries, where each group must travel in different vehicles, sometimes targeted groups tend to sit in only certain seats of buses or trains. While sitting in a café in the 1960s, Jim Wong-Chu overhead an old Chinese gentlemen talking about the railways. The sections of the train that were considered most dangerous were where the Chinese could sit. Jim Wong-Chu turned this story into the following poem.

EQUAL OPPORTUNITY

Jim Wong-Chu

in early canada
when railways were highways

each stop brought new opportunities

there was a rule

> *the chinese could only ride*
> *the last two cars*
> *of the trains*

that is

until a train derailed
killing all those in front

(the chinese erected an altar and thanked buddha)

a new rule was made

> *the chinese must ride*
> *the front two cars*
> *of the trains*

that is

until another accident claimed everyone in the back

(the chinese erected an altar and thanked buddha)

after much debate
common sense prevailed

the chinese are now allowed
to sit anywhere
on any train

THE INTERNMENT OF THE MURAKAMI FAMILY

THE DATE DECEMBER 7, 1941, IS AN IMPORTANT day in history. Early in the morning of that day, Japan attacked Pearl Harbor in Hawaii. World War II was already in its second year, but the attack brought the United States into the war. Canada reacted to the invasion immediately. All Japanese Canadians came under suspicion. In British Columbia, some forty men of Japanese descent were arrested, beginning a series of actions that would be taken against Japanese Canadians. A few months later, on February 26, 1942, the federal government ordered the removal of Japanese Canadians from the West Coast.

Men, women, and children were taken from their homes. They were placed in relocation centres in the B.C. Interior and in other provinces until the end of the war. Their rights of citizenship ceased to exist. In all, 21,000 who claimed Japanese heritage would be forced to leave their homes. These actions are referred to as internment. The forced relocation, separation from family members, and poor living conditions created hardships during those years. For these Canadians, life would never be the same.

Mary Murakami, who was seven at the time, and her family were among the Japanese Canadians who were interned. Her grandfather had immigrated from Japan in 1898 and her grandmother followed four years later. Her mother was born in Canada and married a Japanese man. Mary and her three sisters and brother were born on Salt Spring Island, British Columbia.

Here, Mary describes some experiences of her internment. It was, as Mary says, a walk into hell. Mary's story starts just after Japan bombed Pearl Harbor.

Mary Murakami (front row left) with her siblings and her mother in 1942 in Greenwood, British Columbia. Mary's father was sent to work at the Yellowhead Pass work camp.

We knew something terrible was going to happen to us. It was something you felt immediately. I' ll give you an example of what happened to my sister. As soon as the war started and she went to school the next day, the teachers and students alike accused her of starting the war. They referred to her with the pejorative "Jap." She didn' t have a name all of a sudden; she was "the Jap." On the way home, she was ambushed by boys who had a stockpile of rocks ready for her and they stoned her as far as they could, chasing her until she got home. If the children were doing that, you can imagine where they got the idea.

Within a day we were locked up in our property. We were not allowed to leave. We were taken out of school and were no longer allowed to go to school or church. We were prisoners on our own property.

Interned Japanese nationals and those naturalized since 1922 had to report to the RCMP. Then, on March 17, 1942, came the day we were all dreading. Don' t ask my mother how she was feeling because I think the pain was so great that she becomes voiceless about that day. The RCMP came for my father. I remember before they came my father lined us up in order of our birth in the living room. He shook each of our hands and told us to be good and to help Mom. Then he turned to Mom and shook her hand. That' s the way things were done in the Japanese way. Mom might have shown a few tears, but she remained strong for us.

Then we followed Dad outside. The RCMP, instead of letting my dad walk onto the pickup truck alone, shoved him and poor Dad stumbled as he got onto the back of the pickup truck. They drove him out of our yard. We were running after the truck, waving and waving at him. We just kept waving and waving as if by waving we would stay connected to him and never let go. We didn' t know where he was going. We didn' t know if we were going to see him again. Like a puff of smoke, he just disappeared from our lives.

Thirty-six days later, the rest of the Murakami family was ordered to leave Salt Spring Island. They were al-

FORCED OUT OF BRITISH COLUMBIA

The first Japanese immigrant to Canada, Manzo Nagano, came in 1877. He settled with his wife in Victoria, British Columbia. By the end of the century, there were Japanese immigrants throughout the province engaged in farming, logging, mining, boat-building, and fishing.

Japanese people began coming in larger numbers in the early 1900s. In 1907, eight thousand came. There was resistance against their immigration, so the government said that only four hundred a year could enter the country. By 1921, slightly more than fifteen thousand Japanese lived in British Columbia. When World War II broke out, there were about twenty-three thousand people of Japanese descent in Canada, most of them in British Columbia. Of those, about thirteen thousand had been born in Canada and about three thousand had become Canadian citizens. Most of the rest had lived in Canada for twenty-five to forty years.

During World War II, in which Canada and Japan were at war, action was taken in Canada against the whole Japanese-Canadian community. Issei (first-generation immigrants) as well as Nisei

In December 1941, fishing boats that belonged to Japanese Canadians on the West Coast of British Columbia were seized by the Canadian government.

(second-generation immigrants) were affected. Japanese newspapers and schools were closed. Many businesses were stopped. Companies that traded

lowed two suitcases each, nothing more. A custodian of "enemy property" was appointed to look after the family's property. The Murakami family was sent to a series of camps and farms.

When we left, the custodian put his arms around my mom and assured her that not one chopstick would be removed from the house until we returned. We didn't know at that time that we were walking into hell.

We rejoined my father on August 14th, five months after our forced separation. We moved to another farm, where we became the "yellow slaves" of a farmer who considered us criminals. The shack that he provided had one room, ten by fifteen feet, with one broken-down stove and a dirty bare floor. Father bought lumber to build bunk beds, benches and a table. The flies from the pig pen, just ten feet away, gave the illusion that the colour of the shack was black. Father worked on the farm while Mother tried to deal with the ordeal of feeding us and keeping us clean. The livestock pond was our source of water. My oldest sister worked as a maid for the farmer's wife. Father's health was deteriorating again: the work and living conditions were taking a toll. A request was made to the authorities to relieve us of this ordeal. A representative came and agreed to return us to the camps.

In November 1942 we reached Slocan. After seven days, we were transferred to Popoff, then back to Slocan. There, we shared a tent with three other families for three weeks. Snow was deep. In January 1943 we were in the first group sent to Roseberry. The tarpaper shacks, built row upon row, were not ready for occupancy. The weather was freezing but we were forced to live in them.

Our household belongings were stolen. Our property was gone. Our bank account was frozen. The money from the sale of our harvest and property was given to us in small amounts. We were forced to pay for our own internment.

with Japan were locked up and their assets frozen. Fishing boats were impounded. In January of 1942, all Japanese males aged eighteen or older, about seventeen hundred men in all, were sent to work camps.

On February 26, the government declared a complete evacuation of people of Japanese descent. Many new orders followed the evacuation announcement. Japanese Canadians were not allowed to leave their homes after dark. They could not purchase liquor. Their letters were censored and their long-distance calls monitored. Cars, radios, and cameras were to be given to the police. Japanese-Canadian high school cadets were dismissed and barred from military training at the University of British Columbia.

The Japanese people were first brought to Vancouver's Hastings Park, where they were housed in old livestock buildings. From there, they were shipped by train to various destinations. Some were sent to prison-of-war camps in Ontario. By

During World War II, Japanese Canadians on the B.C. coast were sent by train to internment camps in the Interior or farther east.

After the war, the Murakami family went to Alberta. They worked on a farm, then opened a restaurant. They worked hard and saved their money. In 1954 they decided to return to Salt Spring Island.

The Murakamis were among the few who did return to their pre-war location. Mary's father had a dream that one day he would be able to return to their old home. He also wanted to be near the son who had died and was buried on the island. They were unable to get their old home back, so they settled on another property. Many of the islanders did not want them back, but the Murakamis stayed and began to rebuild their lives.

Mary now lives in Vancouver with her husband. Her brother and two sisters continue to live and work on Salt Spring Island. Mary writes and gives talks about her internment experiences.

In the summer of 1943, the Murakami family was reunited when the father joined them in Roseberry, British Columbia. Mary is standing in the back row, centre.

the end of October most of the Japanese Canadians had been moved to the Interior of British Columbia. Only a hundred tubercular patients were left at Hastings Park. A handful of people—those who had married white Canadians—did not have to go. About eighty others refused to go. One, Yokokichi Isomura, was a veteran of World War I.

As the end of the war approached, the interned Japanese Canadians were given an ultimatum. They could either settle east of the Rocky Mountains or go to Japan. Many did not know where to go. More than four thousand went to Japan after the war ended. The rest headed east. They were banned from the city of Toronto. Churches, and especially Jewish communities, helped many of the Japanese Canadians settle in the east. It was not until April 1949 that they were allowed to return to the West Coast.

Other ethnic groups besides Japanese Canadians have suffered internment in Canada. During World War I, there were twenty-four internment camps in Canada. More than eight thousand people were interned—people with German, Austro-Hungarian, Romanian, Slovak, Czech, Hungarian, Polish, and Ukrainian backgrounds. During World War II, people with Italian and German backgrounds, as well as some communists whose political views were unpopular, were interned.

Japanese Canadians were stripped of their rights and forced to work in work gangs during World War II.

A Dead Village Without Children

THE DOUKHOBORS CAME FROM RUSSIA TO Canada in 1899 to settle in what is now Saskatchewan. Their religion gave them their distinct culture. They believed in communal living, in sharing land and produce, and in peace. They stressed living separately from their neighbours. The Doukhobors came to Canada so that they could have the freedom to live according to their beliefs.

After arriving in Canada, the Doukhobors faced pressure by the government to give up their habits. Over time some did, and the Doukhobors split into two groups. One group joined the larger Canadian society; the others were determined to keep their traditional customs. These Doukhobors became known as the Sons of Freedom.

In the 1950s, a dispute between the government and the Sons of Freedom arose over education. The Sons of Freedom wanted to educate their own children. The government wanted the children to go to public school. In 1955 the government took the Doukhobor children from their homes and placed them in government residential schools.

The following is an excerpt from a story by Vi Plotnikoff. She is of Doukhobor heritage and was a young girl in the 1950s. In this excerpt, a young girl named Lara is telling a friend about the seizure of Doukhobor children and the experience of living in a residential school.

We heard about the children in one of the other villages. About the way the police just drove right in, got out of their cars carrying sticks, walked slowly toward the houses. There were about ten of them. Then the bus drove in. The people had come out of their houses by now, and when they saw the bus, they knew something very terrible was about to happen. Some were in the fields and came running.

The police told the adults to stand to one side, and then lined up the children in a row on the other side, all the ones who looked of school age. The younger ones were clinging to older sisters and brothers. Some had no one to cling to. The door of the bus opened

Conflicting Beliefs

The Doukhobors came from Russia. They were originally peasants from southern Russia. Their religious beliefs can be traced to the 1600s. They believed that God dwells in each person. They rejected the church and government authority, replacing the Bible with their own teachings. They believed that their leader was important and inspired by God. They did not believe in fighting or in wars. They lived in a community, sharing, and helping each other.

In the late 1700s and 1800s this group was persecuted for their beliefs. A church archbishop called them Doukhobors, meaning Spirit-Wrestlers. They adopted this name. They were moved from their homes and resettled. Their leader was exiled. Soon they decided to immigrate to Canada. In 1898 and 1899, seventy-four hundred came to Saskatchewan.

Clashes began between the new immigrants and the government because their ways of living were against some Canadian regulations. New settlers were supposed to own land individually, but the Doukhobors wanted to live in a community. They were required to register all births and deaths, but they also resisted this law. Although the government had promised that the Doukhobors could live in communes and be exempt from military service, it soon changed its mind. When they went to apply for the land on which they had been living, the government refused their application. The government took over half of their land, saying that some of the Doukhobors had refused to swear an oath of allegiance (loyalty), which was necessary to get a homestead title.

and the police herded all the children up the steps.

By this time, the parents and grandparents were crying and shouting, mothers trying to get past the line of policemen, who stood in a row, arms extended at their sides, holding the sticks. They wouldn't let anyone through. The door of the bus closed and the bus rolled away down the hill, and the faces of the children were pressed against the window. It all happened so quickly, the people had no time to do anything. They were too shocked. And then there was nothing but the silence. It was a dead village without children . . .

Soon after that it was my turn. And when it came, it too was a surprise. We thought we were ready, but the real thing is always so different. When the police car drove [into the village] in the morning, I was in the kitchen doing breakfast dishes, my aunt and uncle were harvesting potatoes away from the house, and Petya and Dasha were playing in the yard. I didn't even hear the motor, just the voices, and looked out the window and saw the black and white car and I knew. So I dropped the towel and ran into Petya's room and hid under the trap door.

As I sat there, barely breathing, heart nearly bursting, I could hear the policemen's voices, talking to Petya and Dasha. They were just eight and seven, you know. I kept waiting for Petya to yell for his mother, but all I heard were the men's voices. Then I heard the little ones crying, pleading.

"No. I don't want to go. I want Mama," Petya's voice. And then I heard Dasha cry, "Lara . . . Lara. Help me."

And before I knew it, I was out of that hole and running outside, and the police grabbed me, but not before the little ones threw their arms around me.

We were seated in the back seat with a woman,

Doukhobors eating a meal on board ship while immigrating to Canada in 1899.

and the two RCMP officers sat in front, and as the car rolled through the village, I looked back and saw my aunt running, shouting something. The car speeded up. We were taken to the courthouse and then on to New Denver that same day . . .

We had good food and beds and learned to read and write, but imagine being separated from your family. Living without anyone who cared about you, just your little sister and cousin. And having to look out for them. When I arrived at the dormitory, it was late and they put us to bed. It was a huge building, all one floor. T-shaped, girls on one side, boys on the other. Classrooms and dining hall in the centre. Petya cried because he wanted to sleep with us, but they took him away. He was very quiet after that. Next morning I was taken to see the matron and I was frightened and tried not to let her know how scared I was, so I stared out

A demonstration in front of the Legislative Buildings in Victoria, British Columbia, in January 1954. Sons of Freedom members were protesting against the forced schooling of their children.

About six thousand Doukhobors decided to move to British Columbia. Once they were in British Columbia, they clashed with the government over education. In the early 1900s, the government wanted new immigrants to conform to the main society. Having new immigrants attend public school was seen as the way to achieve this. Some groups resisted. Other religious minorities, such as the Hutterites and Mennonites, thought that having their children attend public school would destroy their ways and customs. The Sons of Freedom, a Doukhobor group determined to keep their own traditions, was the group most affected by this clash over education.

The Sons of Freedom resisted the compulsory attendance at public school. They did not want their children to learn about military history, be involved in military drills, or have competitive tests and grading. They wanted them to learn about Russia, their original homeland. In 1914 the government passed a law making attendance at public school compulsory. In protest, the Sons of Freedom burned down some schools. They staged nude marches (which were sanctioned by their religion) to draw attention to their cause. Close to six hundred men and women were arrested, charged with public nudity and sentenced to three years in jail. Three hundred and sixty-five children of the Sons of Freedom were put in orphanages and homes while their parents were in jail. In 1939 the government of British Columbia seized the land that belonged to the Sons of Freedom.

The Sons of Freedom and the government continued to clash. In the 1950s, when the Sons of Freedom again refused to send their children to public school, more protests began. The government took the children and put them in residential schools.

the window and wouldn't look at her. She thought I was rebellious and gave me a severe scolding about respect and how I should be grateful for this wonderful opportunity, for I would be taught not only reading and arithmetic, but manners. In fact, I'd be exactly like "a well-bred little Englishwoman."

I didn't want to be a well-bred anything, especially an Anglichka. The other girls didn't like me because I was pretty and the boys talked to me. So I had no one except for Dasha and Petya . . .

The visits [from our families] were the best and worst days in our lives. I still have bad dreams. Every other Sunday was Visitors' Day, and oh how excited I was the night before each visit. I couldn't sleep. But with the anticipation was pain. The pain of parting all mixed up with the joy of the visit. We'd be waiting by the fence long before our parents and grandparents arrived with picnic lunches. We'd kiss and touch each other through the wire fence, then stand back and hold a prayer service in Russian, reciting psalms, the Lord's Prayer, sing a hymn. Our mothers would take out the picnic lunch, pass eggs, tomatoes and cucumbers, cheese and bread through the fence. After we ate, we'd talk a little, but we knew the parting was coming fast and we wouldn't see one another for two whole weeks. And as the minutes of the visit quickly wound down, only pain remained until it filled my heart, my very breath, and I'd try to hold back the tears because my mother would be holding back hers. I'd try to be very brave and blink real hard to keep them in the back of my eyes while I kissed my parents through the fence and touched Mama's hand. As they drove away, everyone waved and waved and finally I'd run inside and hide under my bedcovers and cry. Many would have swollen eyes at supper that night.

Vi Plotnikoff now lives in Castlegar, British Columbia. Castlegar is mainly a farming community with many descendants of Doukhobors. Vi continues to write and give lectures on the lives of Doukhobors in Canada.

A mother kisses her child goodbye through the fence at the New Denver Institution for Sons of Freedom children in 1954.

SPIRITS OF THE RAILWAY

THE FIRST CHINESE IMMIGRANTS ARRIVED IN Canada in 1858 at the beginning of the gold rush in British Columbia. The Chinese called their destination Gold Mountain. Thousands worked in the goldfields. When the Canadian Pacific Railway was being extended to the West Coast, many workers were needed, far more than lived in British Columbia at the time. Between 1880 and 1885, about fifteen thousand Chinese men came to British Columbia.

After 1885, the immigration laws for Chinese people became discriminatory. Not only did the Chinese men have to pay a "head tax" in order to come and work in the province, they were not allowed to bring their wives or families with them. Often they would be separated from their families for years. The government wanted workers for the railway, but it did not encourage them to settle in the province. It expected the Chinese men to return to China after the work was completed. Despite the discrimination, many stayed in order to make money, which they often sent home to their families.

The working conditions on the railway were very difficult and dangerous. About fifteen hundred Chinese workers died. Dynamite blasts caused landslides that killed many. Others died because of inadequate living quarters, poor nutrition, and a lack of medical care. Chinese workers were paid only half the wage of White workers.

Here is an excerpt from Paul Yee's *Tales from Gold Mountain*. This book is a work of fiction, but it is based on real events. In this story, a young man named Chu comes to Canada from China to look for his father. His father had left China to work on the railway in the New World. While searching for his father, Chu also starts to work on the railway. He learns of the harsh conditions the workers face, and he meets one of the spirits of the railway.

Many Chinese men who worked on the railway lived in camps such as this one near Kamloops, British Columbia, in 1886.

When the morning mist had lifted, Chu's mouth fell open. On both sides of the rushing river, gray mountains rose like walls to block the sky. The rock face dropped into ragged cliffs that only eagles could ascend and jutted out from cracks where scrawny trees clung. Never before had he seen such towering ranges of dark raw rock.

The crew pitched their tents and began to work. They hacked at hills with hand-scoops and shovels to level a pathway for the train. Their hammers and chisels chipped boulders into gravel and fill. Their dynamite and drills thrust tunnels deep into the mountain. At night, the crew would sit around the campfire chewing tobacco, playing cards and talking.

From one camp to another, the men trekked up the rail line, their food and tools dangling from sturdy shoulder poles. When they met other workers, Chu would run ahead and shout his father's name and ask for news. But the workers just shook their heads grimly.

"Search no more, young man!" one grizzled old worker said. "Don't you know that too many have died here? My own brother was buried alive in a mudslide."

"My uncle was killed in a dynamite blast," muttered another. "No one warned him about the fuse."

The angry memories rose and swirled like smoke among the workers.

"The white boss treats us like mules and dogs!"

"They need a railway to tie this nation together, but they can't afford to pay decent wages."

"What kind of a country is this?"

Chu listened, but still he felt certain that his father was alive.

Then winter came and halted all work. Snows buried everything under a heavy blanket of white. The white boss went to town to live in a warm hotel, but Chu and the workers stayed in camp. The men tied potato sacks around their feet and huddled by the fire, while ice storms howled like wolves through the mountains. Chu thought the winter would never end.

IMAGES OF THE CHINESE

In the 1880s in British Columbia, negative attitudes towards Chinese immigrants increased. In 1884, the government tried to find out more about this problem. It sent questionnaires to various citizens to get their opinion about the Chinese. Some were in favour of Chinese families settling in British Columbia, while others were against it. Sir Matthew Begbie, Chief Justice of British Columbia, and Joseph Metcalf, Jr., returned the following answers. Chief Justice Begbie recognized the contribution that Chinese people were making to the building of Canada; Mr. Metcalf saw them as a threat.

Question: What classes of people come here as emigrants from China?

Begbie: *I would say by far the larger number of them trust to the pick and shovel: either agricultural, or road-making, or mining. Another large class take to domestic service; scarcely any establishment in the province has any other servants. Another large class take to trade. The menial task of washing and of splitting and sawing stove-wood are almost entirely engrossed by Chinamen. They are employed about every building. Every Chinaman in British Columbia has the air of having worked, and of being ready to work.*

Metcalf: *About 95 per cent are labourers, and the other 5 percent are traders.*

Question: Do they often become a burden upon the private charity of white citizens?

Begbie: *I never hear of Chinamen becoming a burden on the private charity of the whites.*

When spring finally arrived, the survivors struggled outside and shook the chill from their bones. They dug graves for two workers who had succumbed to sickness. They watched the river surge alive from the melting snow. Work resumed, and Chu began to search again for his father.

Late one afternoon, the gang reached a mountain with a half-finished tunnel. As usual, Chu ran up to shout his father's name, but before he could say a word, other workers came running out of the tunnel.

"It's haunted!" they cried. "Watch out! There are ghosts inside!"

"Dark figures slide soundlessly through the rocks!" one man whispered. "We hear heavy footsteps approaching but never arriving. We hear sighs and groans coming from corners where no man stands."

Chu's friends dropped their packs and refused to set up camp. But the white boss rode up on his horse and shook his fist at the men. "No work, no pay!" he shouted. "Now get to work!"

Then he galloped off. The workers squatted on the rocks and looked helplessly at one another. They needed the money badly for food and supplies.

Chu stood up. "What is there to fear?" he cried. "The ghosts have no reason to harm us. There is no reason to be afraid. We have hurt no one."

"Do you want to die?" a man called out.

"I will spend the night inside the tunnel," Chu declared as the men muttered unbelievingly. "Tomorrow we can work."

Chu took his bedroll, a lamp, and food and marched into the mountain. He heard the crunch of his boots and water dripping. He knelt to light his lamp. Rocks lay in loose piles everywhere, and the shadowy walls closed in on him.

At the end of the tunnel he sat down and ate his food. He closed his eyes and wondered where his father was. He pictured his mother weeping in her bed and heard her voice calling his father's name. He lay down, pulled his blankets close, and eventually he fell asleep.

Chu awoke gasping for breath. Something heavy

Metcalf: *They do not become a burden upon private charity of white citizens.*

Question: Are they industrious, sober, economical and law-abiding, or are they lazy, drunken, extravagant or turbulent?

Begbie: *Lazy, drunken, extravagant, and turbulent: this is, by the voices of their friends and foes, exactly what a Chinaman is not. This is, on*

Many Chinese men worked as miners in British Columbia. Here a gold miner is working in the Cariboo region in the province's Interior.

Chinese immigrants provided much of the labour for building the Canadian Pacific Railway in Western Canada in the nineteenth century.

the whole, *I think, the real cause of their unpopularity. If Chinamen would only be less industrious and economical, if they would but occasionally get drunk, they would no longer be the formidable competitor with the white man which they prove to be in the labour market; there would be no longer a cry for their suppression.*

Metcalf: *Chinamen are industrious when working for themselves, but lazy when working for others. They are too economical, as they hoard all their money up and send it home to China.*

Question: When the Chinese first came to this province, did they supply a want then felt, and was their coming encouraged and welcomed?

Begbie: *They certainly supplied a want then felt. But I do not think they were ever much encouraged.*

Metcalf: *They supplied no want, but took the places of white people, who had to leave the district. Their coming was discouraged and protested against by 98 per cent of the people.*

Question: Has the presence of Chinese contributed to the development of the province and is their presence here any longer necessary or desirable?

Begbie: *As to the past, the undoubted facts are: First, that Chinamen are very largely, and till within a year, mainly, employed in all laborious parts of our coal mines. Second, they constitute three-fourths of the working hands about every salmon cannery. Third, they are a very large majority of the labourers employed in gold mining. Fourth, they are the model market gardeners of the province, and produce the greater part of the vegetables grown here. Fifth, they have been found to be absolutely*

was pressing down on his chest. He tried to raise his arms but could not. He clenched his fists and summoned all his strength, but still he was paralyzed. His eyes strained into the darkness, but saw nothing.

Suddenly the pressure eased and Chu groped for the lamp. As the chamber sprang into light, he cried, "What do you want? Who are you?"

Silence greeted him and then a murmur sounded from behind. Chu spun around and saw a figure in the shadows. He slowly raised the lamp. The flickering light traveled up blood-stained trousers and a mud-encrusted jacket. Then Chu saw his father's face.

"Papa!" he whispered, lunging forward.

"No! Do not come closer!" The figure stopped him. "I am not of your world. Do not embrace me."

Tears rose in Chu's eyes. "So, it's true," he choked. "You . . . you have left us . . ."

His father's voice quivered with rage. "I am gone, but I am not done yet. My son, an accident here killed many men. A fuse exploded before the workers could run. A ton of rock dropped on us and crushed us flat. They buried the whites in a churchyard, but our bodies were thrown into the river, where the current swept us away. We have no final resting place."

Chu fell upon his knees. "What shall I do?"

His father's words filled the tunnel. "Take chopsticks; they shall be our bones. Take straw matting; that can be our flesh. Wrap them together and tie them tightly. Take the bundles to the mountain top high above the nests of eagles, and cover us with soil. Pour tea over our beds. Then we shall sleep in peace."

The immigrants of the 1800s had to work in difficult jobs when they first came to Canada. They found work in railways, mines, construction, sawmills, or factories—places where they did not need to speak English or have special training. Working conditions were hard for all, and discrimination against certain immigrant groups made the conditions even harder. Chu's account gives an idea of the struggles that some of the early Chinese immigrants endured. After the railway was finished, many Chinese workers went to work in West Coast canneries and saw-

---

indispensable in the construction of the railway. Sixth, they are largely, sometimes exclusively, employed in nearly every manufactory or undertaking of any description.

I do not see how people would get on here at all without Chinamen. They do, and do well, what white women cannot do, and do what white men will not do.

Metcalf: *It has prevented white men with families from coming here. In other words, if British Columbia had not here 12,000 Chinese, she would have had some 24,000 more of white population, and this would have made the province a flourish-* ing place. Their presence is not necessary. The industries can afford to pay for white labour, and have reasonable profits.

Question: Has white immigration been retarded by the presence of Chinese immigrants in this province?

Begbie: *I cannot believe that it has. Chinamen are employed not so much because their normal money tariff is lower than the whites—and yet not much lower; many Chinamen get thirty dollars, and some even thirty-five dollars and forty dollars per month—as because they are, as a rule, more sober, steady, docile and industrious.*

Metcalf: *Yes. White people will not care to come to a province where there are Chinese to compete with and live in their midst.*

These two views were expressed over one hundred years ago. The questionnaire was about the Chinese, but it could refer to any group that differs from the majority. It would be a mistake to think of Mr. Metcalf's comments as ideas that belong to the past or that solely concern Chinese people; many of his ideas are still held today by one group against another.

For many years Chinese men were not allowed to bring their wives and children to Canada. Here are Chinese children in the town of Barkerville, in the Cariboo region of British Columbia, at the turn of the twentieth century.

mills. Others became gardeners, shopkeepers, restaurant owners, or peddlers.

Paul Yee found that many older Chinese people want to forget the early bad times, but he believes their stories should be told. The bad times, as well as the good, have shaped the character of Canada. These early Chinese workers, he says, have a claim to be known as pioneers.

Paul Yee is a third-generation Chinese Canadian. He recognizes that despite his family's history in Canada and its contributions, he, and Chinese people in general, are still seen as foreigners and newcomers. He continues to write books about the experiences of the Chinese people in Canada.

FIVE

Weaving a Country

The story of immigrants to Canada is a story not only about people, but also about what people bring with them. Over generations, immigrants have come with plants, animals, foods, and cultural traditions. They arrive with their old ways, but gradually adopt the customs of the new land. Sometimes when old meets new, something uniquely Canadian emerges.

To the new immigrant, Canadian culture seems new, but it has actually developed over time from the traditions of many other groups. Aboriginal people and immigrants from all over the world have contributed to what we now think of as Canadian culture. Each custom that is part of our Canadian identity has its own unique and rich story—and each contributes to the weaving of a country.

In this chapter, Kathryn tells us about her life on Vancouver Island, British Columbia. As she describes her life—where her ancestors lived, her family's Christmas celebrations, her pets, and sports she enjoys—we see that familiar things in her everyday life have evolved from surprisingly varied origins. Kathryn's story points the way for you to research the foods, plants, animals, and customs that are part of your family's or your community's heritage.

As immigrants spend time in their new land, the land itself gradually becomes part of their identity. Immigrants live with and adjust to the lakes, trees, mountains, and snow—until these elements become part of their lives. In the following poem, David Bouchard tells of the impact the land had in making him who he is. He was born on the Prairies. All the characteristics of Prairie life—the dark winter sky, the winds and snow, trips to the hockey rink—made him different from people not born on the Prairies but a kindred spirit with other Prairie people. Across Canada, the land shapes the people.

PRAIRIE BORN

David Bouchard

And the prairie continues to live in my heart
It's much more than memories that tell me apart
It's the wind and the sun, the cold and the snow
Only things that a child of the prairie will know.

If I had a penny for each time I spoke
Of cold howling winds, of deep drifting snow
Of darkness of winter on route to the rink
Of so many memories, I smile to think.

It shapes us from childhood through sun and through
rain
Compels us to live for life's pleasures and pain
And the secret of me from the day of my birth
Is the nurturing seasons and rich prairie earth.

You see . . .

My hair's mostly wind, my eyes filled with grit
My skin's white then brown, my lips chapped and split
I've lain on the prairie and heard grasses sigh
I've stared at the vast open bowl of the sky
I've seen all the castles and faces in clouds
My home is the prairie and for that I am proud.

KATHRYN'S CONNECTIONS TO THE PAST

TODAY LIFE IN CANADA IS A MIXTURE OF OLD customs and new ways. As each generation passes, more and more changes take place. The following personal profile by Kathryn Cook illustrates the mixing of old and new ways. At the time she wrote it, Kathryn was a fifteen-year-old high school student living on Vancouver Island, British Columbia.

Kathryn's story helps us understand the adventures of those who came before her. Her ancestors all contributed to who she is now, but so did many other groups who also came to this land. Some of Kathryn's ancestors were in the first groups of immigrants to come to Canada—the French, and Scots in Nova Scotia. Other ancestors came from Ireland and, via the United States, from Germany.

The influences of many groups are seen in Kathryn's life. The food she eats, her two cats, and the sports she likes originate in immigrant cultures. Kathryn's story is one story of the weaving of a country.

I was born in Grande Prairie, Alberta, on June 20, 1983. . . . The earliest recollection I have is when we moved to Cowichan Station on Vancouver Island when I was two . . .

We first lived in a tiny, two-room house on twenty-one acres. My parents cleared the land and built our house made of wood from the trees on the land. My father also built a workshop to do his business. The house is in a secluded property with woods and fruit

CATS FROM AFAR

The varied origins of Kathryn's cats show how not only people but also animals have "immigrated" to Canada. Billy is a grey Persian. Persian cats were introduced to Europe from Afghanistan, Iran, Turkey, and Russia in the 1600s. Before that time there were no long-haired cats in Europe. An Italian writer, Pietro della Valle, was the first to bring cats with long silver-grey hair from Persia (present-day Iran) to Europe. These cats were originally only for the aristocracy (upper classes). Years later, European immigrants introduced Persian cats to Canada.

Kathryn's other cat is a Himalayan. Despite its name, this breed of cat is a Siamese version of a Persian. It has long hair like a Persian, but the blue eyes and light colouring of a Siamese. It is named after the Himalayan rabbit that has the same colouring. The Himalayan breed as it is now known was bred at the Harvard Medical School in the United States in 1935.

Long-haired cats such as this blue-and-white Persian were introduced to Europe from Iran and Afghanistan, and years later emigrated from Europe to Canada.

This memorial church and museum in Grand-Pré, Nova Scotia pays tribute to the thousands of Acadian people who were deported beginning in 1755. It is part of the Grand-Pré National Historic Site of Canada.

trees we planted. In the pastures the deer and rabbits are often seen roaming through the land and occasionally we have a bear or cougar move on through. It is like a fantasy land. We have two cats. One is a Persian called Billy, and his mother is a Himalayan called Danielle . . .

Last summer my poppie [grandfather] died and Nannie [grandmother] decided we should take a trip to Nova Scotia where she grew up. So in July, Nannie, Mom, and I left by plane from Vancouver to Halifax. . .

CHRISTMAS IN CANADA

Christmas traditions in Canada have developed from a variety of sources. The Christmas tree as a holiday symbol originated in Germany. The custom of gift giving can be traced back to the Egyptians, who exchanged charms or tokens for good luck at the end of the year. Although the exact origin of the custom of hanging Christmas stockings is uncertain, many believe it developed in Holland, where children set their shoes by the chimney at night to be filled with presents before the next morning.

Christmas foods also come from different sources. Fossil evidence shows that turkeys lived in the Americas ten million years ago. Early colonists on the east coast found an abundance of wild turkeys in the forests. They used turkey in the first Thanksgiving meal, and adopted it to replace the traditional festive dish of goose, peacock, or swan at Christmas. Today all turkeys bred in the world are descendants of the North American wild turkey. They were

Early immigrants began to domesticate wild turkeys, which were native to North America.

introduced to Europe in 1530 from North America, but have never been as popular in Europe as they are in Canada.

Squash is another food native

We visited relatives I had never seen before. We saw the church in Evangeline with stained glass pictures of the expulsions of the Acadians ... We also went to Pictou county to see where our relatives from Scotland first settled in the early 1600s ...

Here Kathryn writes about some of her family's traditions, her hobbies, and her history. As she learns more about her family's past, she can see the links to her own life.

Christmas is a special time every year. We wrap our presents, pack the car, and go to Nannie and Poppie's in Vancouver. When we arrive the tree is up and deco-

Kathryn Cook hanging a Christmas stocking at her grandparents' home.

The squash family of vegetables is native to North America. Squash have become part of Christmas and Thanksgiving dinners for many immigrants.

to North America that has become part of many Christmas celebrations in Canada. In 1605 Samuel de Champlain recorded in his journals that aboriginal people on the east coast grew many squashes and pumpkins, as well as corn, beans, and tobacco. From wild squash a great many kinds of squashes have been developed, including summer and winter varieties with various shapes and colours.

Christmas cake comes from the English plum pudding. The pudding was solidified and made without alcohol so that it was suitable for family teas. Shortbread is a Scottish pastry that has become a Christmas staple in Canada. Chocolate is another food commonly associated with Christmas. The story of chocolate in the Americas predates Columbus. Chocolate is made from the bean of the cocoa plant, and it was used by the aboriginal people of Central America and Mexico as a healing tonic. The Spanish explorer Cortez, who visited that part of the world, introduced cocoa beans to Spain. From there cocoa spread to Europe and England, and in the early 1700s chocolate made its way to the colonies in North America with Dutch immigrants. From this brief history we can see that many cultures have contributed to the chocolate that is enjoyed at Canadian Christmas festivities.

rated and Nannie has made shortbread cookies and Christmas fruit cake . . . In the evening we have our Christmas dinner. All the family come so we have about thirteen people. We have turkey, dressing, gravy, mashed potatoes, Brussels sprouts, carrots, beans, squash, and for dessert we have marshmallow delight. Mom and Nannie help make the dinner and my dad carves the turkey. We always have wine and a toast to the family and to a happy year ahead.*

. . . I like sports. I play baseball, soccer, and swim, and I used to skate . . . Poppie said he used to play baseball on the Prairies when he was a boy. His family came to Canada in 1834 from Ireland . . . My dad's family are also from the Prairies. They settled on the Prairies in the 1870s. They were French from Quebec. They were the original settlers along the Saskatchewan River in a village named Lamoureaux after their family, which was

Immigrants from many countries have brought their love of soccer to Canada.

WORLD SPORTS

The sports that Kathryn enjoys have many different origins. Baseball, although commonly seen as an American game, evolved from the English game of rounders. That game in turn evolved from stick-and-ball games that were played for recreation and used as part of certain ceremonies in ancient cultures in Persia (Iran), Egypt, and Greece. This type of game spread throughout Europe by the Middle Ages (5th century to 15th century), and Europeans brought stick-and-ball games to North America as early as the 1600s.

Kicking games that were the forerunners of soccer and football were also played in many ancient cultures. The modern game of soccer began in 19th century England, where a variety of football games had developed, all of which involved both handling and kicking a ball. In 1863, in England, the game of football was divided into rugby football (the parent sport of North American football), and association football, known in North America today as soccer. The major difference between the two sports is that soccer banned the use of the hands.

British traders, sailors, and immigrants introduced soccer all over the world, and today the World Cup championship soccer tournament is the world's most popular sporting event. In Canada, as of 1998, more men and women are participating in amateur soccer than in hockey. This growth in soccer's popularity is thanks to immigrants from many countries

across from Fort Saskatchewan. Dad's mother's family came to the Prairies in the early 1900s from America. They were of German ancestry.

I am learning more about my ancestors and just gave a presentation at school on this topic. It gives me more of an understanding of who I am and where my roots are.

What we know as Canadian culture—our music, art, dance, sports, languages, and literature—is woven from countless immigrant cultures. Out of many traditions, new and old, a uniquely Canadian culture continues to emerge. If you take the time to research your own family history and traditions, you too can share in the pride of weaving a country.

Two young figure skaters in bell-hop costumes at the Rotary Ice Carnival in Vancouver in about 1948.

who have brought their love of the game to their new country.

Swimming was highly esteemed in ancient Greece, Egypt, and Rome, especially as a form of training for warriors. In Japan, swimming competitions were held as early as the first century B.C., and in 1603 swimming became part of the education program throughout the country. Competitive swimming began in Great Britain in the 1830s, and soon after the sport was introduced to Canada by British immigrants. Amateur swimming clubs were organized as early as the 1870s in Montreal and Toronto.

Ice skating has been practised in Northern Europe for centuries. In early times the ribs or shinbones of animals were bound to the feet, and skaters glided on these by propelling themselves with the aid of a spiked stick. Later, iron or steel blades were introduced, and both speed skating and figure skating became popular. But it was a young American ballet dancer, Jackson Haines, who blended ballet music with skating to introduce modern figure skating in the 1860s. Ice skating and hockey are major sports in Canada, in part because the cold winter climate in most regions of the country allows for outdoor skating rinks where young people can learn these sports.

GLOSSARY

adapt: change or adjust to new conditions. Immigrants had to adapt to different lifestyles in Canada.

adopt: to choose to take over or use something as one's own. To fit into Canada, many immigrants adopted different styles of dress and customs.

ancestor: a person from whom one is descended, such as a mother, father, grandfather, or grandmother.

basic freedoms: In Canada, all people have certain basic freedoms. Some of these are freedom of thought, speech, and religion, and the right to peaceful assembly.

civil war: a war between the citizens of the same country, state, or community. In the Vietnam War, the communists who were in control of North Vietnam were fighting to take over the government in South Vietnam.

compulsory: something that is required by law or a rule. In Canada, education is compulsory, and each province sets the ages children must attend school (usually 6 to 16), and what they have to study.

concentration camp: a prison camp for the detention or mass killing of political prisoners of war (people seen as enemies of the government) and interned foreigners.

consulate: the residence and offices of a person (consul) who is appointed by a government to look after its business in a foreign city. Consulates usually supply visas to people wanting to visit their countries.

culture: the overall way of life of a group of people. Culture includes a group's shared values and beliefs; their roles, behaviours, and ways of interacting with others; their social systems and structures, and their creations. Culture is used in the general sense to mean those who belong to the same ethnic community.

custom: the accepted way of acting in a community; a tradition. Many customs are part of celebrations and festivals of communities.

deport (deportation): to banish or expel. When a person is deported, he or she is sent out of the country, usually back to his or her native land.

Depression (The Great): a 10-year period starting in 1929 in which millions of people in North America had no jobs. Many people lost their homes or farms and had to move far away.

descendant: a person who can trace his or her parentage to a certain individual family or group. All people in Canada are descendants of immigrants except for First Nations people.

discrimination: actions that withhold rights, privileges, and power from some groups and individuals while giving them to others. Discrimination is sometimes part of law, such as the head tax charged to Chinese immigrants in certain years.

dominant: a group in a society with the most influence and power, which gives it the control to impose its ideas on others.

emigrant: a person who leaves his or her own country to live in another country. A person emigrates from his or her own country to another. In the country the person comes to, he or she is called an immigrant.

environment: physical surroundings, conditions, and circumstances in which a person lives and works. The environment influences how a person lives. Many immigrants to Canada faced hostile land and unfriendly people in their environments.

equality: the same, equal, or balanced in terms of rights and rewards for individuals or groups. In Canada today, equality is guaranteed for all under the law regardless of race, ethnic origin, colour, religion, sex, age, or disability.

ethnic (community): a group of people with a shared racial, historical, geographical, social, and language background. An ethnic community is often associated with race, nationality, or religion.

generation: all the people born about the same time. A generation is usually considered about 30 years—the average time from the birth of one generation to the birth of another.

ghetto: a part of a city in which a minority is forced to live because of poverty, prejudice, or government policy. In the Warsaw ghetto, 400,000 Jews were forced to live in an area of 9 square kilometres surrounded by a 3-metre fence.

head tax: a tax levied on new immigrants to a country. The Chinese were the only group to be charged a head tax to come to Canada. The head tax was legal racial discrimination.

heritage: things such as works of art, cultural achievements, and folklore that have been passed on from earlier generations. Heritage can be anything that is handed down to a person from his or her ancestors, whether it is something physical or ideas or beliefs.

Holocaust: the organized killing of over six million Jews and other "undesirable" people by the Nazi government in Germany before and during World War II.

intermarriage: marriage between members of different religious, social, or ethnic groups.

internment (internment camps): forced to stay in a certain place, especially during a war.

immigrant: a person who is living in a country other than where she or he was born and who may not yet be a citizen. Generally this term is used to describe people who are in a country on a long-term basis and intend to make it their home. Immigrants are allowed into a country by the government, which sets up conditions under which they may come. These conditions may change from time to time and from group to group.

multicultural: refers to two or more cultures. Countries like Canada are multicultural because the people living in them represent many cultures.

naturalize: to give citizenship of a country to someone from another country. Many Canadians are naturalized citizens.

persecution: to treat badly or do harm to someone, especially for religious, racial, or political reasons.

prejudice: dislike or distrust of a person or group based on ideas and beliefs rather than on objective facts and current information.

prison camp: a camp for political prisoners (people who the government says are its enemies) or prisoners of war (people who have been captured in a war).

racial (biracial): a term used to identify human groups with hereditary physical differences such as skin colour, facial features, and body characteristics. The concept of human races was developed approximately 200 years ago, and today race is considered a very imprecise term. Biracial refers to a relationship between two people of different races.

refugees: people who have left their homeland because of war, famine, or other dangers. The rules for letting refugees into a country are different than those for immigrants. Refugees are usually evaluated by the dangers they would face if they returned to their homelands.

refugee camp: a camp where refugees stay until a country will accept them or until they can go back to their own country. There are approximately 39 million people living in refugee camps in the world today.

residential schools: boarding schools operated or funded by the federal government for students who must attend classes far from their homes. Residential schools in Canada were mostly for First Nations and Inuit children.

rights of citizenship: as a citizen, each Canadian has certain rights. Some of these are: the right to vote or to be a candidate in elections; the right to enter, remain in, or leave Canada; the right to earn a living and live in any province or territory; the right to a fair trial; and the right to protection against discrimination.

segregate: to separate groups and individuals in social or economic (working) life based upon beliefs of superiority/inferiority regarding religion, race, or class. Segregation can be informal or based in law.

suppression: to put an end to something or stop by force.

tradition: an established belief, custom, practice, story that is handed down from one generation to another.

utopia: a perfect place in which everyone is equal and lives in harmony, and where there is no social injustice.

World War II: a war fought from September 1, 1939 to August 14, 1945 mainly in Europe, Asia, Africa, and at sea. The Axis Powers (German, Italy, and Japan) were defeated by the Allied Forces, which eventually included the United Kingdom, Canada, Australia, New Zeland, the United States, and the Soviet Union.

CREDITS

The publisher wishes to thank the following sources for photographs, illustrations, and other material reproduced in this book. Every effort has been made to determine and locate ownership sources of copyrighted material. We will gladly receive information enabling us to rectify any errors or omissions in these credits.

The following abbreviations are used to credit sources:

BCA — British Columbia Archives
NAC — National Archives of Canada
UBC Archives — Special Collections and University Archives Division, University of British Columbia
UNHCR — United Nations High Commissioner for Refugees
USHMM — United States Holocaust Memorial Museum

PHOTOGRAPHS/ILLUSTRATIONS

Contents page

From top to bottom: courtesy USHMM; Richmond Chinese Community Society; NAC, PA 186957; Glenbow Archives, NA-387-27; City of Vancouver Archives, #1194-2472

Introduction

p. 4, Courtesy UNHCR
p. 5, Courtesy BCA, PN E-03019

Chapter One

p. 8, Painting by Francis Hustwick, courtesy New Brunswick Museum, #985.19
p. 9, Courtesy Norah Bastedo
p. 10, Courtesy NAC, C-004986
p. 12, Photo by Louis Gonda, courtesy USHMM
p. 13, Courtesy Susan Bluman
p. 14, Top, courtesy Susan Bluman; bottom, courtesy Visas for Life Foundation
p. 15, Courtesy Visas for Life Foundation
pp. 16, 17, and 18, Courtesy UNHCR
p. 19, Photo by John Denniston/The *Province*

Chapter Two

p. 22, Courtesy Edinburgh City Libraries
p. 24, Painting by J. E. Woolford, courtesy Nova Scotia Museum
p. 25, Courtesy Town of Pictou, Nova Scotia, Department of Recreation, Tourism and Culture
p. 26, Courtesy Glenbow Archives, NA-303-252
p. 28, Courtesy BCA, D-04655
p. 29, Top, courtesy City of Vancouver Archives, CH P86 N125; bottom, courtesy UBC Archives, neg # BC 489/4
p. 30, Photo by George Hunter, courtesy NAC, PA 123476
p. 32, Courtesy Sesquicentennial Museum and Archives, Toronto District School Board
p. 34, Courtesy Hong Kong Economic and Trade Office, Vancouver
p. 35, Courtesy Richmond Chinese Community Society
p. 36, Courtesy Hong Kong Economic and Trade Office, Vancouver
p. 37, Courtesy Richmond Chinese Community Society

Chapter Three

p. 40, Photo by Anderson, courtesy BCA, E-03019
p. 42, Courtesy UBC Archives, neg # AIKA SPAM 1/4C
p. 43, Courtesy BCA, D-08473
p. 44, Courtesy Pauline Foggo
p. 46, Courtesy Glenbow Archives, NA-769-6
p. 47, Courtesy Cheryl Foggo
p. 48, Courtesy Librairie à la page Saint-Boniface
p. 49, Painting by Azor Vienneau, courtesy Nova Scotia Museum, #12212
p. 50, Courtesy Provincial Archives of Manitoba, N 8888
p. 51, Top, courtesy NAC, PA 186957; bottom, courtesy NAC, NL 18232
p. 52, W. J. Sisler Collection, 118, courtesy Provincial Archives of Manitoba, N 9631
pp. 53, 54, and 55, Courtesy Muryl Anderson

Chapter Four

p. 58, Courtesy Mary Kitagawa
p. 59, Courtesy NAC, PA 134076
p. 60, Courtesy UBC Archives, neg # XI-3
p. 61, Top, courtesy Mary Kitagawa; bottom, courtesy UBC Archives, neg # V-15
p. 63, Courtesy BCA, C-01435
p. 64, Courtesy BCA, C-01740

p. 65, Courtesy BCA, C-01724

p. 66, Photo by Edouard Gaston Deville, courtesy BCA, D-04707

p. 68, Courtesy BCA, A-05056

p. 69, Photo by Boorne and May, courtesy Glenbow Archives, NA-387-27

p. 71, Courtesy BCA, C-09457

Chapter Five

p. 74, Photo by Jim Brown, courtesy Gail Boden and Wendy Trottier

p. 75, Top, courtesy Grand-Pré National Historic Site of Canada; bottom, courtesy NAC, C-007787

p. 76, Top, courtesy Jerry Robinson; bottom, courtesy Catherine Edwards

p. 77, Courtesy Stephen Edwards

p. 78, Courtesy City of Vancouver Archives, #1184-2472

TEXT CREDITS

Chapter One

p. 7, "The Cuban Emigrant," by Victor Alvarez, is reprinted by permission of Dutton Children's Books/Penguin Putman Inc. from *Here I Am!,* copyright 1969 by Virginia Olsen Baron.

pp. 9–11, excerpt from the journal of Eleanora Hallen is reprinted by permission of Scholastic Canada Limited from *Eleanora's Diary,* copyright 1994 by Caroline Parry.

pp. 12–15, excerpts in "Susan's Visa" are reprinted by permission of the Vancouver Holocaust Education Centre from the exhibition "Visas for Life" by Frieda Miller, copyright 1996 by the Vancouver Holocaust Centre Society.

pp. 17–19, excerpt in "Nam's Journey to Canada" is reprinted from *A Boy Called Nam,* copyright 1984 by Leo Heaps.

pp. 17–18, excerpt in "A Letter Home" is reprinted from *Letter to Vietnam,* copyright 1980 by Eugene Buia.

Chapter Two

p. 21, "From Shovel to Self-Propelled Snow Blower: The Immigrant's Progress," by Rienzi Crusz, is reprinted by permission of the author. Copyright 1996 by Rienzi Crusz.

pp. 22–25, excerpt in "The Pictou Highlanders' First Year" is reprinted by permission of Natural Heritage Books from *Scotland Farewell,* copyright 1996 by Donald MacKay.

pp. 23–24, excerpt in "Do You Have the Gaelic?" is reprinted by permission of Doubleday Canada/ Random House of Canada Limited from *Voice of the Pioneer,* copyright 1988 by Bill McNeil.

pp. 27–29, excerpt in "Voices of Pioneer Sikhs," by Sarjeet Singh Jagpal, is reprinted by permission of the author from *Becoming Canadian,* copyright 1994 by Sarjeet Singh Jagpal, published by Harbour Publishing.

pp. 30–33, excerpts in "First at Bat in a New School" and "A Birthday List" are reprinted by permission of Penguin Books Canada from *Small Mercies: A Boy After War,* copyright 1997 by Ernest Hillen.

pp. 34–36, excerpts in "Letter to a Friend" and "Astronaut Families" are reprinted by permission of C.B.C. British Columbia.

Chapter Three

p. 39, "My Genealogy," by John Robert Colombo, is reprinted by permission of the author. Copyright 1976 by John Robert Colombo.

pp. 41–43, excerpt in "Sointula: Dreams of Utopia" is reprinted by permission of the British Columbia Archives from the Aural History Programme, "Arvo Tynjala. The Finnish Community at Sointula, B.C.," by Imbert Orchard, copyright 1967 by the British Columbia Archives.

pp. 45–47, excerpts in "Hairday: Pressing Identity into Submission" and "An African Ancestor" are reprinted by permission of Detselig Enterprises from *Pourin' Down Rain,* copyright 1990 by Cheryl Foggo.

pp. 48–51, excerpts in "Crossing the Provencher Bridge" and "The Acadians" are reprinted by permission of Patricia Claxton, translator, from *Enchantment and Sorrow,* by Gabrielle Roy, published by Lester, Orpen & Dennys, 1987.

pp. 53–55, excerpt in "Heritage Lost and Found" is reprinted by permission of the author from "How I Became Ukrainian," copyright 1997 by Muryl Anderson.

p. 53, excerpt in "What's in a Name?" is reprinted by permission of the author from *The Forbidden City within Victoria,* copyright 1991 by David Chuenyan Lai, published by Orca Book Publishers.

Chapter Four

p. 57, "equal opportunity," by Jim Wong-Chu, is reprinted by permission of the author.

pp. 59–60, excerpt in "The Internment of the Murakami Family" is reprinted by permission of the author, Mary Kitamura, and C.B.C. British Columbia.

pp. 62–65, excerpt in "A Dead Village without Children" is reprinted by permission of Raincoast Books from *Head Cook at Weddings and Funerals,* by Vi Plotnikoff, copyright 1994 Raincoast Books.

pp. 67–68, 70, excerpt in "Spirits of the Railway" is reprinted by permission of Groundwood Books/ Douglas & McIntyre Ltd. from "Spirits of the Railway" in *Tales from Gold Mountain,* copyright 1989 by Paul Yee.

pp. 67–70, excerpt in "Images of the Chinese" is reprinted from Canada, Sessional Papers, 1885, No. 54a "Royal Commission on Chinese Immigration."

Chapter Five

p. 73, "Prairie Born" is reprinted by permission of Orca Book Publishers from *Prairie Born,* text by David Bouchard, illustration by Peter Shostak, copyright 1997.

pp. 74–78, journal excerpts by Kathryn Cook are reprinted by permission of the author.

INDEX

Other titles in the Alternatives to Racism series from Pacific Educational Press are:

Folk Rhymes from Around the World
ISBN 0-88865-081-7

Folk Rhymes from Around the World Teacher's Guide
ISBN 0-88865-083-3

A Handbook for Enhancing the Multicultural Climate of the School
ISBN 0-88865-025-6

The Tale of a Silly Goose and Other Stories
ISBN 0-88865-082-5

The Tale of a Silly Goose Teacher's Guide
ISBN 0-88865-084-1